OUR LADY SPEAKS

Thoughts on Her Litany

by

LÉON BONNET

Translated by
Leonard J. Doyle

A GRAIL PUBLICATION

St. Meinrad   Indiana

NIHIL OBSTAT:
  JOSEPH G. KEMPF, PH.D.
    Censor Librorum

IMPRIMATUR:
  ✠ PAUL C. SCHULTE, D.D.
    Archbishop of Indianapolis

Feast of St. Anne
July 26, 1954

Library of Congress Catalog Number 54-11419

i

CONTENTS IN LOGICAL ORDER

Our Veneration of Mary

MEDITATIONS FOR THE FEASTS OF THE BLESSED VIRGIN

November 21, *Presentation*: Virgin of virgins; Queen of virgins; Queen of Apostles.

December 7, *Vigil of the Immaculate Conception*: Unsullied Mother; Faithful Virgin; Health of the sick.

December 8, *Immaculate Conception*: Queen conceived without original sin; Mystical rose; Mirror of justice.

December 15, *Octave of the Immaculate Conception*: Mother most pure; Mother most chaste; Tower of ivory.

From *Christmas* to *Epiphany*: Mother of the Creator; Mother of the Savior; Pray for us.

February 2, *Purification*: Queen of confessors; Seat of Wisdom.

February 11, *Apparition of the Immaculate Virgin*: Mother ever virgin; Ark of the covenant.

March 25, *Annunciation*: Virgin worthy of all praise; Spiritual vessel.

July 2, *Visitation*: Mother of divine grace; House of gold.

July 16, *Our Lady of Mount Carmel*: Powerful Virgin; Clement Virgin.

August 5, *Our Lady of the Snows*: Mother of good counsel; Tower of David.

August 14, *Vigil of the Assumption*: Queen of all saints; Vessel of honor; Virgin most prudent.

August 15, *Assumption*: Queen taken up into heaven; Queen of angels; Queen of patriarchs.

August 22, *Immaculate Heart*: Lovable Mother; Venerable Virgin; Famed vessel of devotion.

September 8, *Nativity*: Cause of our joy; Morning star.

September 12, *Holy Name*: Holy Mary; Help of Christians.

September 15, *Seven Sorrows*: Queen of martyrs; Comforter of the afflicted.

September 24, *Our Lady of Mercy*: Mother of Christ; Refuge of sinners.

October 7, *Most Holy Rosary*: Queen of the most holy rosary; Queen of peace; Queen of prophets.

October 12, *Motherhood*: Holy Mother of God; Admirable Mother; Gate of heaven.

Note

Throughout this book the Blessed Virgin herself is considered to be instructing and exhorting the reader. This is only a literary device, of course. Its aim is twofold: first, to sustain the soul's attention and fervor by having it hear a cherished voice at every moment; then, to keep arousing the soul to answer its heavenly Mother with praise, supplication, outpourings of thanks and of love ... and also with confessions, regrets, promises. ...

Perhaps certain readers will be shocked to hear the humble Mary praising herself. Let them recall that silence about the gifts of God is a law of exile: the law of the Fatherland desires their proclamation.

With better reason, others will disapprove the very notion of having the Blessed Virgin speak. Let them be indulgent toward a fiction from which little souls may draw benefit, and which may help themselves to become better established in that attitude of a child without which no one can enter the kingdom of heaven.[1]

[1] *Matt.* 18:3.

The title of the original work is: O VIERGE MARIE, Elevations sur les Litanies de la Sainte Vierge by Pere Leon Bonnet. Published by Bonne Presse, Paris, 1952.

HOLY MARY

MARY, OUR TRUE MOTHER

W HY is it, my child, that all truly Christian souls experience such joy and delight on hearing the name "holy Mary"? Why does it arise so readily in their minds, in their hearts and on their lips? Is it because Mary may signify either Power or Light or Beauty (your scholars are not agreed)? No, it is simply because that name calls to mind your "heavenly Mother."

The Church teaching proclaims with one voice that I am the true Mother of men, as far as their supernatural life is concerned. In her liturgical prayer the Church says, "Lord Jesus, You have made Your Mother our Mother."[1] Through the voice of Pius XII she teaches "that she who was bodily the Mother of the Head became spiritually the Mother of all His members."[2] So speaks the Church teaching.

Such also is the common belief of the Church taught. From the great saints who spend their lives meditating my privileges down to the little child who hardly knows how to babble my name, all believe with unshakable faith that I am a true Mother, and they turn eagerly to my motherly love, as a

[1] Collect of the Mass of Mary Mediatrix of All Graces, May 31.
[2] *On the Mystical Body,* #110.

1

plant turns toward the sun, to receive light and warmth from it!

Since the Universal Church cannot err, it is therefore beyond doubt that I am your Mother. But *in what does this mother-hood consist?* To be a mother by adoption means to bestow one's name and inheritance on another's child and to lavish on him a devotion and love similar to that of mothers. To be a mother in the proper sense means essentially to transmit life.

Now just as the fruit tree is capable of two lives—that of the wild stock which can produce only bitter fruits and that of the graft which uses the sap of the wild stock to draw delicious fruits from it—so every man is called to receive two lives: first, that of nature, which produces acts sometimes good, sometimes bad, but always without any value to merit heaven; then, that of grace, which, by supernaturalizing your purely human activity, makes it divine and enables it to merit the inheritance of the children of God.

In order to bring men to birth in supernatural life, God has made me a partner with Christ, the new Adam.

The Word made flesh has begotten all men into the life of grace through the merits of His life, consummated by the supreme merit of His death. For this merit enables men to receive the Holy Spirit, principle of supernatural life, as generation enables a portion of matter to receive the soul, principle of natural life: "He gave them power to become children of God."[3]

I collaborated with Him in this great work by meriting for all men, in equity, that supernatural existence, that divine life

[3] *John* 1:12.

which He was meriting for them in justice. Such is the teaching of Saint Pius X: "Associated by Christ Himself in the work of saving humanity, she merits for us in equity what Christ merited in justice."[4]

That is how I am the true Mother of your life of grace, your supernatural life.

At what moment did I become your Mother? Since I begot you into supernatural life by meriting it for you through Jesus and with Jesus, the *stages of my spiritual motherhood* coincide with the stages of my merit as Co-Redeemer.

The merit begins with the "Fiat" of the Annunciation; for as soon as my "Behold the handmaid" is united with the "Behold I come" of Jesus, He begins to merit the life of grace for you.

It continues throughout Christ's earthly existence; for through Him and with Him I offer to God at every moment a new merit on behalf of all men.

It is consummated by the "Fiat" on Calvary, which marks the final achievement of my merit as Co-Redeemer. And that is why Jesus chooses this hour for the solemn promulgation of my spiritual motherhood: "Woman, behold your son!—Son, behold your Mother."[5]

Whose Mother am I?

As spiritual motherhood consists essentially in meriting the life of grace, and as I have merited that life for all men, I am *the Mother of all,* even of those who lived before me;

---

[4] *Ad diem illum,* Feb. 2, 1904; translated by the Rev. George D. Smith in *Mary's Part in Our Redemption* (New York: P. J. Kenedy & Sons, 1938), p. 81.
[5] *John* 19:26-27.

for God, who sees the future as the present, can have regard for a future merit.

Nevertheless, I am in a way doubly the Mother of the faithful of the new Law, because, after acquiring the life of grace for them on earth, I have received in heaven the mission of dispensing it to them.

Of each of them I can say that I conceive him, I carry him, I give birth to him, as I have conceived, carried and given birth to the Mystical Body in its entirety.

I conceive him when I procure his baptism, which deposits in him, in germ, the divine life of grace, supernatural existence. I carry him all during his earthly existence by dispensing to him at all times the graces designed to protect that germ, to nourish it, to make it unfold towards its full flowering. I give birth to him by obtaining for him a holy death, which introduces him into life eternal and blessed.

Do you want to glimpse *the excellence of that spiritual motherhood?* Consider how it surpasses bodily motherhood.

The life it communicates to you is incomparably more perfect, a life capable of being renewed many times, a life whose least degree is worth more than all the goods of nature put together, a life which makes you the equal of angels, the brother of Christ, the child of God, a life which the dying breath does not extinguish, but on the contrary causes to open out into life eternal.

My spiritual motherhood involves more costly sacrifices than natural motherhood, since I had to deliver my Jesus to death in order to let you be born into supernatural life; and this was harder for me than to deliver myself to death.

Spiritual motherhood is accompanied by cares more constant and more prolonged; for, from your baptism until your
entrance into heaven, I keep surrounding and nourishing your
supernatural life, causing it to increase, in a sort of ineffable
pregnancy.

Above all, spiritual motherhood is accompanied by a motherly love incomparably greater than that of bodily motherhood.
For God the Father, having adopted you as His children,
Himself conferred on me a mother love worthy of your condition as child of God, worthy of your supernatural life. God
the Son, having incorporated you into Himself as His true
members, urges me to extend to each one of you that unspeakable motherly tenderness which I have for Him. And the
Holy Spirit, having given me the mission of revealing to you
His infinite love, poured out into my heart alone more tenderness than He poured into the hearts of all mothers together.

Since I am a true Mother to you, *you must behave towards
me as a true son.*

To that end, it is not enough that you show me in ideal
form the deference, the gratitude, the affection which you
ought to have for your mother here below; you must take
the filial devotion of Jesus towards me and make it your
own. Contemplate often, therefore, how respectful and obedient He was to me, how considerate and thoughtful, how
tender and devoted; and strive to imitate Him.

And as you will soon feel yourself incapable of reproducing a Model so sublime, do not grow tired of begging Him to
make you participate more every day in His indescribable
filial love for me. In this way you will respond to the most
ardent desire of His divine Heart!

HOLY MOTHER OF GOD

EXCELLENCE OF MARY'S DIVINE MOTHERHOOD

T HE gospel, my child, affirms with equal clarity that Jesus is my Son and that Jesus is God. Bringing together these two affirmations, Christian tradition has concluded very justly that *I am the Mother of God.*

When the impious Nestorius denied the validity of this conclusion, the Council of Ephesus condemned him as a heretic and solemnly proclaimed, with the approval of the Christian world, that I am truly "Mother of God, because I gave birth to the Word of God made flesh."

To be sure, in the Word made flesh I produced only the body and by no means the soul, created by God alone, nor yet the divine nature and Person, which exist from all eternity.

But in order to be anyone's mother it is required and it is sufficient to have begotten his body. Now the body which I conceived, carried and brought forth is truly the body of the Word, the Son of God. For, from the very first moment of its existence, that body was assumed by the Person of the Word in such a way that it belongs to Him as really as the body born of Elizabeth belongs to John the Baptist. In John the Baptist it is God alone who created the soul and brought

6

about that union of soul and body from which the human person results; Elizabeth produced only the body. Nevertheless, that which is her son is not John's body but John himself. Similarly, that which is my Son is not the body of the Son of God but the Son of God himself.

What is *the greatness of this dignity* of Mother of God? Listen to what the greatest theologians think of it.

For St. Anselm, it is the greatest favor that may be granted a mere creature: "Wonder of wonders! . . . There is nothing equal to Mary; only God is greater than Mary."[1] For St. Bonaventure "one can conceive nothing more sublime."[2] For St. Thomas Aquinas "it is a dignity in a way infinite."[3]

You may, however, form some idea of it by comparing it with the other dignities of earth or heaven. What are kings and popes in comparison to Christ? and even the heads of the nine choirs of angels? All of them are no more than His servants, while I am His Mother. In the mind of God as in the opinion of men, the mother of a prince is incomparably higher than his servants, of whatever rank they may be; this is so true that all, even the highest of the seraphim, owe me reverence and obedience.

You may get some idea also of the esteem in which God Himself holds this dignity by considering *what graces He assigns to it* as preparation or crowning; for, being supremely wise, He always proportions the means to the end, the honors to the dignity.

---

[1] *Oratio 52, ad S. Virginem Mariam;* in J.-P. Migne, *Patrologia Latina* (Paris), vol. 158, col. 956.

[2] *In I Sent.,* d. 44, dub. 3.

[3] *Summa Theologica,* I, q. 25, a. 6 ad 4um.

To make me worthy of this divine motherhood, He is not content with preserving me from all original and personal sin, from every inclination to sin, from every imperfection (something He has not done for any other child of Adam); He has heaped upon me from the very first instant of my conception a fulness of graces, virtues and gifts greater than those He reserves for angels and men together.

Then, to honor this unique dignity as it deserves to be honored, He places on my brow a crown of unique privileges: on earth, virginal motherhood, collaboration in the work of redemption, assumption; in heaven, reign over all creatures, universal dispensation of graces, right to a worship of hyperdulia.

Finally, you may glimpse even more easily the greatness of this motherhood by considering in what a *close* and absolutely unique *union* it ties me *with the three divine Persons,* source of all greatness.

With regard to the Son, I filled all the functions of a mother towards her child.

Because the Word appropriated to Himself, from the first instant, the body which was born of me, it follows that all the services and all the devotion I lavish on that body are directed to the Word Himself. At sight of this the angels, carried away in admiration, could say in all truth: "How great is she who encloses in her womb Him whom the universe cannot contain! who feeds with her milk Him who feeds all the living! who carries in her arms, sustains, protects Him who is infinite Power! who guides, instructs, counsels Him who is infinite Wisdom!"

Similarly, with regard to the Word made flesh I have all

the rights of a mother over her child. Throughout His life, indeed, Jesus showed me a real filial love and gratitude, deference and obedience. No doubt these various duties spring from His human heart. But, as the Word has taken that heart for His own, with all the feelings of which it is the source, it is really the Word Himself who shows me those sentiments!

And here again the angels, ravished with admiration, contemplate the sovereign Majesty surrounding me with all sorts of considerations and attentions! the Angel of the great counsel and sovereign King of the universe following my advice and carrying out my commands! the supreme Good of men and angels shutting Himself up for nine months in my womb and for thirty years in my house, as if He belonged to me alone! finally, supreme Love showing me His affection like a little child who needs a constant exchange of embraces and caresses.

But this unequaled intimacy with the Son wins for me in its turn *a unique love* on the part of the Father and of the Holy Spirit.

The Father and the Spirit love a creature in the measure in which it resembles the incarnate Word, the supreme Exemplar in whose image everyone was created. Now I am the living copy of Him in soul as well as in countenance: I alone reflect His beauty better than all the angels and saints together. And that is why the Father and the Spirit are more pleased with me than with all of them.

In the second place, the affection of the Father and of the Spirit for a creature are proportioned to the love which that creature gives to the incarnate Word and the love it receives from Him. Now, make no mistake, all the love which the dwellers in heaven give to Jesus or receive from Him is truly inferior to that which I give Him and that which I receive from Him.

These considerations give you a glimpse of the greatness of my divine motherhood. In order to have a sensible image of it, call up the great vision of the Apostle: "A woman clothed with the sun, and the moon under her feet, and on her head a crown of twelve stars."[4] The fondness of the elect raises me, as it were, on a pedestal; the admiration of the angels encircles my brow with a crown of light; the love of the Trinity, enveloping me in its radiance, makes me more resplendent than the sun!

Together with me, my child, often thank the Most High for having chosen me to be the Mother of His Son, and make it your aim to show me on every occasion the respect, the admiration, the confidence to which such a high dignity lays claim.

[4] *Apoc.* 12:1.

HOLY VIRGIN OF VIRGINS

TRANSCENDENCE OF MARY'S VIRGINITY

I AM the Virgin of virgins, my child, because I possessed in a transcendent way *the virginity of the body.*

Other virgins have preserved, as have I, their bodily integrity. But I am the only one in whom virginity did not exclude motherhood. How could a favor as eminent as the divine motherhood have been the occasion for any loss to my body? Death itself was unable to bring into it the least germ of dissolution: the great disrespecter treated my body with a great respect, content with extinguishing its perishable life so as to let it receive a life immortal and blessed.

I am the Virgin of virgins because I possessed in a transcendent way *the virginity of the senses.*

The most vital concern of virgins is to preserve themselves from sensual love. But if they succeed in denying it the access of will and consent, still they cannot prevent its befouling mists from infiltrating into their imagination or their feelings, so as to make them say, "Who will deliver me from this body of death?"[1]

As for me, far from ever consenting to the suggestions of lust, I never felt them. The world and the devil could besiege my interior or exterior senses with their most disturbing images; they were powerless to awaken there even a little con-

---

[1] *Rom.* 7:24.

cupiscence, for the very simple reason that concupiscence never existed there, even in germ, such as it exists in a newborn infant.

When there are no dregs in a vessel, it may be shaken in every direction without clouding the water contained in it. Now in me there were never any dregs.

I am the Virgin of virgins because I possessed in a transcendent way *the virginity of the heart,* characterized by the exclusion of all division and all hesitation between the love of God and the love of creatures.

Thrown into space, straw and stone are both drawn towards the center of the earth, but with unequal force. In renouncing everything, virginal souls throw themselves, in a way, into the void, to be drawn more effectively by God, their Center, their All, their sovereign Good. And what represents here the force of the attraction or of the heaviness is the love which they have for God and which God has for them: "My love is my weight," says St. Augustine.[2]

The love of other virgins being relatively feeble, their movement towards God is, like that of the straw, constantly slowed down and turned aside. Since my love, on the contrary, is greater than that of the angels and the saints, I have always tended towards God, like the stone towards the ground, without pause, without digression, and with more speed the nearer I approach that sovereign Good.

I am the Virgin of virgins because I realized in a transcendent fashion *the mission God assigns to virgins.*

By their purity of soul and body they are to make Jesus forget the flood of luxury which submerges the world; by

[2] *Confessions* 13:9.

their delicate, undivided love they are to console Him for the universal forgetfulness and ingratitude. Now my purity shines with such splendor and my charity burns with such a flame that I procure for Him incomparably more joy and give Him incomparably more love than all other virgins together.

With regard to men, virgins are to obtain indispensable grace for them by the exceptional favor they enjoy with God and, at the same time, make them esteem and cultivate that grace by the attractiveness of their own lives, embellished with the reflection of God. But, while this sanctifying influence of other virgins extends only to a very limited portion of time and space, mine extends to men of all ages and all countries; for there is not one of them who does not receive some grace, and it is I who obtain it for them and dispense it to them.

Finally, I am the Virgin of virgins because I have received the mission and *the power of raising up virgins* in the Church of Christ.

Through my merits and my prayer I obtain for them that very special grace without which no one can conceive or realize the plan of consecrating her virginity to God.

By my example, my provocation, my love, I incite in them the courage to correspond to that grace. My very image is productive of purity: it has no sooner appeared, a radiant sun, on the threshold of a soul than it drives away from that soul all the mists brought on by concupiscence.

The fact is that before my day it was hard to find six virgins (six vestals) in the whole Roman empire, but I bring them to light by hundreds of thousands in each new generation. For it is really true that Agnes and Cecilia, Teresa of Avila and Therese of Lisieux, and all the other virgins, are my work before being my ornament. I am the great fleur-de-lis; they are the ornaments, sprung from my stem, fed by my pith, borrowing from me that whiteness and that perfume which ravish the heart of the divine Spouse.

What an enviable role! Of all the divine favors which it is my mission to dispense, *the grace of virginity* is truly one of the most precious.

If I come one day, then, to offer it to you, my child, welcome it with gratitude and follow its promptings with generosity.

It will ask that you make a pact with your eyes to shut them to the lying allurements of creatures, but it will win for you the reward of opening them wide, one day, and satiating them in the home of eternal Beauty.

It will ask that you deprive your heart of all earthly love, but it will win for you the reward of being steeped one day in the very sources of eternal Love and, even now, it will make you worthy of being loved by that which is most loving and make you capable of loving that which is most lovable, namely God, Christ, your Mother and your brethren of paradise, all the redeemed souls.

Finally, if it demands that you forswear all earthly motherhood, this is in order to make you worthy, through a life more pure and loving, of a motherhood infinitely more noble, one which gives souls birth into life eternal; so that when you step across the threshold of paradise, it will win for you the joyful surprise of seeing your children run to meet you and throw themselves into your arms—true offspring, more loving and more numerous than those which bodily motherhood gives.

MOTHER OF CHRIST

MARY CO-REDEEMER

S T. PAUL tells you, my child, that Jesus is the only Mediator between God and men. What grounds have the doctors of the Church, then, for giving me the title of Co-Redeemer?

I contribute to your redemption, first *by giving you the Redeemer*. For Him you are indebted to me, after God.

The eternal Father was ready to bestow on men that ineffable gift which was His own Son. But He did not want to force the gift on them; it had to be desired and implored. Now the human race for thousands of years had sent up in vain the tears of the unhappy, the remorse of sinners, the sighs of the just: it was still far from attaining the measure of desire and supplication demanded by God.

It was I who filled up that measure, in a few years, by the endless flow of prayers that surged from my heart, renowned vessel of devotion.

The Son was willing to become the Head and Savior of men by putting on a human nature. But in the course of all the generations He had not yet been able to find a Mother suited to Him: a Mother whose body was pure enough to transmit to Him a flesh free from all evil heredity, whose soul

15

was holy enough to be worthy of loving a Child-God like a mother and being loved by Him as by a son.

Then I appeared among the daughters of Eve like a lily in the midst of thorns, immaculate, resplendent with grace, on fire with love. I answered so fully the desires of the Word and attracted Him so irresistibly that He came down without delay from the bosom of the Father into my virginal womb.

The Holy Spirit was willing to fashion a body for the Man-God out of my chaste blood. But as it would be completely unworthy of Him and of me that He do this without my knowledge and against my will, He sent me an angel to propose that I become the Mother of the Redeemer. And the incarnation would not take place until I gave this message the assent of my faith and the acquiescence of my will.

That assent gained great merit. A virginal conception, a God becoming flesh in a human nature—what unheard-of mysteries! What docility to the word of God was required for immediate, unhesitating belief!

The consent of my will gained still greater merit. To become Mother of the Savior (I knew by the prophet) was to become Mother of Him whose hands and feet would be pierced and whose bones would be numbered.[1] It was to bear, to nurse, to deliver to the torturers the Victim who would expiate the sins of the world; it was, in consequence, to become a victim with Him.

Through love for you, I gave that "Fiat" which was holding the whole redemptive plan in suspense. And thus, thanks to me, the human race came into possession of the Savior so long awaited. Hence the liturgy sings this praise: "Behold,

[1] *Psalm* 21:17-18.

Mary has brought forth unto us a Savior.[2] By her we deserved to receive the Author of life."[3]

Not only did I give you the Author of the Redemption, but *I was associated in the whole span of the redemptive work.*

Begun from the first moment of the Incarnation, this collaboration was pursued throughout the earthly career of Jesus and consummated on Calvary.

To have some notion of it, consider in the first place that the Holy Spirit had so welded and identified my soul with that of Jesus that it vibrated in unison with His, spontaneously and in all things.

As a lyre causes another to reverberate with it when tuned exactly to itself, Jesus made me partake of all His plans, all His concerns, all His affections.

Wholly enflamed with the love of God and of men, He enkindled that twofold flame in me. Grief-stricken at the sight of the outrages done by sin to God and the damage done to souls, He made me feel the same suffering. Undertaking all labors, accepting all trials with a view to procuring reparation for sin, He inspired me at every moment to do everything and suffer everything with the same intentions.

Thus from His Incarnation to His Passion He caused me to make satisfaction and to obtain merit, through Him and with Him, on behalf of all men.

Still the divine plan required that the redemptive work *would be completed only through* the supreme satisfaction and merit of the sacrifice of *the cross.* I took part in that sacrifice.

[2] 5th antiphon at Vespers of the Circumcision.
[3] Collect *Deus, qui salutis aeternae.*

During the Passion I was immolated with Jesus. That gentle Son could have kept me far from Calvary and ignorant of everything. But, since He called me to the foot of the cross and made me see, through the eyes of the body and those of the soul, all His interior and exterior sufferings, it was impossible that I should not myself undergo all the phases of the martyrdom I was witnessing; that I should not feel the sting of the lash, the piercing of thorns and nails; the shame of the mockeries, the blows and the spittle; the bitterness of the flood of ingratitude and hatred that was overwhelming Him.

Victim immolated with Jesus, I was also a victim offered with Him and by Him. Knowing that my martyrdom was the inevitable result of His, He could not consent to His martyrdom without consenting to mine; indeed both were proposed to Him inseparably united, and He acquiesced to both.

Knowing that I was feeling and taking to myself His sufferings, as He was feeling mine and taking them to Himself, He united both in a single offering of reparation and redemption. The drop of water mixed with the wine becomes an integral part of the oblation of the altar; my martyrdom, mingled with that of Christ, became an integral part of the oblation of the cross.

Finally, I cooperated in offering the sacrifice. My will was one and the same with that of Jesus: to consent to His immolation and to mine with the same sentiments of perfect obedience to God, sovereign Master, and of perfect love for God, sovereign Good. My intention was one and the same with that of Jesus: to offer His immolation and mine so as to obtain adequate reparation to God for all sins and to merit for men a superabundance of pardon and of grace.

In the Mass the Church appropriates and offers, in the name of all her members, the interior sacrifice of Jesus, which applies the fruits of the Redemption.

On Calvary I was the only one to know, the only one to appropriate and to offer, on behalf of all men, the interior sacrifice of Christ, which was effecting the Redemption. Thus, as Pius X teaches, by this union of suffering and of will, I deserved to become the Restorer (*reparatrix*) of the lost world.[4]

By this you see how I am the only Co-Redeemer in the strict sense. Through their satisfaction or their merit, all the other members of the mystical body, however holy they may be, concur only in the dispensation of pardon and of grace. To me alone was it given to concur in their acquisition.

But Jesus remains nonetheless the unique Redeemer; all my power to merit and to satisfy for men issues from His and depends on it, as a branch on its trunk.

For what reasons did Jesus want to associate me in His redemptive work? First of all, to add luster to His revenge on the devil: a woman contributed to Satan's victory, a woman will contribute to his defeat; a woman contributed to the fall of the human race, a woman will contribute to its redemption.

He willed it further out of mercy for me, to procure for me the signal honor of collaborating in the salvation of all, thus winning eternal praise and recognition from all. Finally, He willed it out of mercy for you, to procure for you, on the

---

[4] *Ad diem illum;* in *Mary's Part in Our Redemption,* p. 81.

level of grace as on that of nature, the smile, the embrace, the tender care of a Mother who loves you intensely because you have cost her so dearly.

Often recall, my child, the part I took in the Redemption. I knew that the stain of sin was making you abominable in God's sight. To cleanse you of that stain, I consented to see Jesus shed all His blood, and myself to shed all my tears.

I knew that your soul was shackled by evil inclinations and chained by Satan on the edge of the abyss. To break those shackles and those chains, I consented to see Jesus nailed to the cross, and to be nailed there with Him myself through the intensity of my compassion.

Finally, I knew that your poor soul was dead to the spiritual life and lying in the corruption of sin as Lazarus lay in the corruption of the tomb. To bring you back to the life of grace, I consented to see Jesus delivered to the most cruel, shameful death, and to deliver myself to an agony worse than death.

Yes, meditate the sorrowful mysteries, persevere in contemplating my unutterable devotion, and you will soon feel your heart on fire with hatred for sin, with gratitude and affection for me.

MOTHER OF DIVINE GRACE

MARY, MEDIATRIX OF ALL GRACES

O N earth, my child, I was associated with Jesus to acquire every pardon and grace for you; in heaven I remain associated with Him to dispense all those pardons and graces to you.

Only the Holy Spirit can infuse or increase in a soul that divine life and beauty which constitute habitual grace; only He can diffuse in a mind or a will the light or the force from on high which constitutes actual grace.

But He can decree, and He has in fact decreed, to give His grace to a soul only in so far as I shall desire it and ask it for that soul; and this is the essence of my universal mediation, with which I want to make you better acquainted.

My intercession on behalf of the bride and bridegroom of Cana will help you understand *my intercession on behalf of each one of you.*

Clear-visioned, I foresaw the unexpected humiliation awaiting that couple. In the same way I perceive in the light of God not only your least prayers and desires, but also the perils and troubles that threaten or weigh down your poor soul unknown to you.

Compassionate, I was moved to pity at the approaching embarrassment of my friends. Since my compassion is active as well as tender, I sought to spare them by turning to Jesus: "They have no more wine."[1] In the same way, in heaven, I am touched by your guilty, unhappy souls, and I keep begging my divine Son to grant them pardon and grace.

All powerful over the Heart of Jesus, I obtained His intervention, even at the price of a miracle, on behalf of the friends I wanted to protect. In heaven I have the same influence to obtain all that is necessary or useful to your welfare.

To be sure, all the saints are permitted to intercede for their brethren on earth, but this is a purely gratuitous privilege. Moreover, their intercession extends only to certain persons, and must still pass through my mediation.

As for me, it is in virtue of an official function, entrusted me by infinite mercy, that I intervene on behalf of all men, to obtain all graces for them.

And here is how that intervention takes place. Either you pray to me yourself and I transmit your prayer to Jesus by making it mine; or you pray directly to Jesus, and I join my prayer to yours; or you pray to a saint, and that saint confides your request in me, that I may present it to Jesus; or you do not pray at all, and in my motherly compassion I ask of Jesus at least the most indispensable graces for you, and first of all a grace that will make you have recourse to prayer.

Thus for whatever grace you receive you are indebted to a triple love: the love of my maternal heart, which begged it for you from Jesus; the love of the Heart of Jesus, which,

[1] *John* 2:3.

through pity for you and regard for me, begged it of the Father; the love of the Father, source of all grace, which poured it into your soul despite your unworthiness, in consideration of the merits of the Redeemer's prayer, but also, secondarily, of the merits of the Co-Redeemer's prayer.

But what proof is there that *this is a certain truth,* not a pious supposition? There is the common belief of the Church, expressed by her doctors, her popes, her liturgy.

Listen to the teaching of the Fathers summed up by St. Bernard: "It is the will of God that we receive every grace through Mary. . . . God has placed in Mary the fulness of all goods, so that all hope, all grace, all salvation come to us from her."[2]

Listen to the teaching of the doctors and the theologians: "All the graces of the Holy Spirit," says St. Bernardine of Siena, "are distributed through Mary to whom she will, when she will, as she will, as much as she will."[3]

Listen to the teaching of the popes. Benedict XIV: "Jesus is the source of all graces; Mary is the heavenly stream through whom they flow down to us."[4] Leo XIII: "Of the immense treasure of graces acquired by the Savior, there is not one which does not have to be dispensed to us by Mary."[5] Pius X: "Mary

[2] *Sermon for the Feast of the Nativity of the Blessed Virgin Mary,* #7 and #6; in *P. L.,* vol. 183, col. 441; in *St. Bernard's Sermons for the Seasons and Principal Festivals of the Year* (Westminster, Md.: The Newman Press, 1950), vol. 3, pp. 288 and 287.

[3] *Sermo* 5; in *Opera Omnia* (Paris), vol. 4, p. 93.

[4] *Gloriosae Dominae* (Sept. 27, 1748); in *Mary's Part in Our Redemption,* p. 157.

[5] *Octobri mense* (Sept. 22, 1891); in *Mary's Part in Our Redemption,* p. 157.

is the Almoner of all the graces which Jesus earned for us by His blood."[6]

Listen, finally, to the teaching of the liturgy in the office of Mary Mediatrix of All Graces: "Christ, the Redeemer, who has willed that we receive all graces through Mary, come, let us adore."

> "Task sublime to no one but Mary given,
> She it is who this sacred wave doth pour out
> At her discretion.
> To us grace and merit of our Redeemer,
> All through Mary, Mother of God, are given."[7]

Why did the divine Savior want me to intervene thus in the dispensation of all graces? He had reasons of wisdom, of justice and of mercy.

Wisdom. Being the new Eve, I should concur in the work of your salvation, as the old Eve concurred in the work of your perdition. With Adam and through Adam she had a share not only in meriting for you the spiritual death of original sin but also in transmitting it to you. To be her living antithesis I must do my part, with Jesus and through Jesus, not only in meriting spiritual life and grace for you but also in transmitting it to you.

Justice. Is it not equitable that I share in the dispensation of divine graces, since I have acquired a sort of co-propriety over them by meriting them all with a merit of equity? Is it not equitable that, having been there for the pain, I should

---

[6] *Ad diem illum;* in *Mary's Part in Our Redemption,* p. 158.

[7] Invitatory and hymn at Matins; translated in *Roman Breviary in English* (New York: Benziger Brothers, Inc., 1951), Spring vol., appendix, p. (6).

also be there for the honor? that, having been associated on earth with the laborious and sorrowful phase of your Redemption, I should be associated in heaven with the glorious and blessed phase? If it is true that nothing cost me so much as to acquire pardon and grace for you, nothing is sweeter to me than to dispense them to you.

Above all, *mercy.*

Pardon and grace must be implored; and often, appalled by your own uncleanness or your ingratitude, you dare not appeal with confidence to Jesus; for if He made Himself your Brother, still He remains your God; if He made Himself your Savior, He remains your Judge.

On the other hand, whatever your sins may be, you are not at all uneasy about appealing to me with full confidence. "Why," asks St. Bernard, "should human frailty fear to approach Mary? In her there is nothing frightening, everything agreeable."[8] Am I not a fond sister to you, a Mother wholly lovable and wholly loving, and moreover a Mother of mercy, having received from God Himself the mission of consoling you, defending you, reconciling you with Him, never of condemning or punishing you?

It is true that you must correspond to grace and that your weakness can hardly adjust itself to the demands of grace. Then it is I who will adjust grace to your weakness, by dispensing it to you in a motherly way, accommodated to your small capacities: to the littleness of your mind, so nearsighted with regard to supernatural realities; to the littleness of your heart, so poor in devotion; to the littleness of your

[8] *Sermon for the Sunday within the Octave of the Assumption,* #2; in *P. L.,* vol. 183, col. 430; in *St. Bernard's Sermons for the Seasons and Principal Festivals of the Year,* vol. 3, p. 259.

will, so inconstant and so timid: "Whosoever is a little one, let him come to me."[9]

Make a resolution, then, my child, to thank the Savior often for the great mercy He has shown you in confiding to me the dispensation of all His graces. Resolve to thank me often, too, for my constant interventions to obtain those graces for you in abundance, despite your unworthiness. Resolve to make all your prayers and all your offerings pass through me, that God may accept them despite their little worth.

[9] *Prov.* 9:4; Common of feasts of the Blessed Virgin Mary, 1st nocturn, 3rd lesson.

MOTHER MOST PURE

MARY PRESERVED FROM ALL PERSONAL SIN

W HY do Christians call me "most pure"? Because, unlike the other children of Adam, I was preserved from everything that could defile a soul.

To be defiled is to come into contact with something baser than oneself: gold does not tarnish the mouth, the mouth tarnishes gold.

Sin defiles the soul. By sin the soul, itself immortal, clings to a perishable good; itself spiritual by nature and by grace, it clings to a sensual good.

Now whereas other souls, even the holiest, cannot long travel the dusty, muddy paths of this world without at least being soiled by venial sin, I was preserved, throughout my earthly pilgrimage, *from the dust of venial sin* as well as *from the mud of mortal sin.* Never did the least adherence to the goods of this world enter in to retard my flight towards the sovereign Good. Never did the least infiltration of the love of creatures mix itself in my heart with the living water of pure Love.

That is a truth of faith, mentioned by the Council of Trent, which did no more than confirm the unanimous belief of the Christian centuries, already so forcefully attested by St. Augustine: "I do not admit that there be any question of the Virgin Mary when we are speaking of sin!"[1]

The same abundance of graces which preserved me from all sin, mortal or venial, also *kept me from all imperfection,* voluntary or involuntary.

Voluntary imperfection implies an opposition of the will of man to the will of God, not to His orders but to His desires. Now my will was so respectful of the will of this sovereign Master and so in love with the will of this tender Father that the mere idea of such opposition really horrified me!

Was He proposing a task for me to fulfill? Without finding out whether it was an order or a desire, I would welcome either one with equal reverence, I would execute either with equal love, a love so total that I never refused Him the least bit of attention, affection or service which the grace of the present moment allowed me to give Him.

Was He imposing a trial for me to undergo? I would not merely accept it, resigned, uncomplaining, without sinful recrimination; I would acquiesce in it with my whole spirit as in an infinitely just decree of my sovereign Master; I would abandon myself to it with all my heart as to an infinitely merciful design of my sovereign Good.

Thus there was never in me any voluntary imperfection, because never for a moment did my will stop adjusting and identifying itself with the divine will, rule of all perfection.

[1] *De Natura et Gratia,* ch. 36, #42; in *P. L.,* vol. 44, col. 267.

Neither was there *any involuntary imperfection.* The greatest saints are subject, in spite of themselves, to distractions and irreverences in their relations with God, to forgetfulness and lack of consideration in their relations with their brethren, to improvidence and blunders in the execution of their charges.

By the superabundance of His gifts and His lights, the Holy Spirit always preserved me from these failures of judgment or of memory, which, although not voluntary and not culpable, nonetheless constitute an irregularity in the sight of God and of His angels.

The greatest saints remain subject likewise to the first movements of the evil inclinations: vanity, sensuality, anger, laziness and so forth. If these last assaults of their old man become less perceptible from day to day and never succeed in forcing the door of consent, they still keep disturbing the senses, the imagination, and even the spirit.

As for me, not only did I never consent to any unruly tendency, but I never felt any, for my senses were as strictly docile to my reason as my reason was to God.

Thus when this thrice holy God examines the temple of my soul, He finds there neither shadow nor dust. When He searches my heart, He sees there no smoke of self love mingling with the pure fire of divine love. When He examines all my other powers, He discovers in them neither blemish nor break.... No weed has come to mingle with the seed of graces with which He has sown them. No grain of that precious seed has failed to germinate and give fruit a hundredfold.

You are right in proclaiming me purer than the saints, since I never committed either sin or imperfection. But because

I was, moreover, happily powerless to commit them, you must proclaim me *purer than the angels,* who during their time of trial were submitted to that possibility and that risk.

And here is the source of my *glorious impeccability.*

First of all, God invested my intellect with a light so intense and so penetrating that it dissipated in an instant all the delusions paraded before me by the tempter. In this brilliance, temptation appeared to me as the worst of follies, since it urges one to sacrifice an eternal good for a perishable good; the worst of injustices, since it suggests the preference of our petty creature will to the sovereign will of the Creator; the worst of ingratitudes, since it asks us to outrage or to sadden the Spirit of love. Thus unmasked, could temptation inspire anything in me but supreme contempt?

At the same time God had set my heart on fire with such a love that every earthly affection which tried to approach that glowing hearth was either reduced to nothing or changed into divine love. And this love carried me along with such impetuosity towards the sovereign Good that the attraction of earthly joys could neither retard my flight nor alter the course of my journey towards God.

With me, *admire and praise* that ineffable love of the Word, enveloping me on all sides as with a wall of fire which it was impossible for the darkness of mortal sin, the fog of venial sin or the shades of imperfection to break through.

But also, in the light of my ideal purity, *be aware* of the multitude of venial stains which bespatter you almost at every step. Is there indeed one exercise of piety in which you do not commit some irreverence? Is there a conversation, a meal, a recreation in which you do not give any food to vanity and sensuality? And do you fulfill one duty of your state without allowing some irregularity to creep into the intention, some negligence into the execution? Now every one of these faults, of which you make so little, still does great injury. Because it tarnishes the purity of your soul, venial sin renders it less worthy of divine favors; because it is a concession made to vanity or sensuality or laziness, it strengthens those various inclinations.

Convinced that in the supernatural order you are but a little one, weak and improvident, always exposed to being soiled, torn, wounded, keep *imploring my motherly assistance* by constant prayer and deserving it by a truly filial devotion.

In return, I will arouse in your soul, by my example and by my grace, an instinctive horror of the least faults, a constant vigilance to repel the least temptations, an untiring courage to mortify the inclinations which give rise to them. And if sometimes I see your path become too muddy, I will not hesitate to preserve you from all defilement by carrying you in my arms as a mother carries her baby.

MOTHER MOST CHASTE

MARY, MODEL AND SOURCE OF CHASTITY

M Y chastity is so pre-eminent, my child, that it has been an object of joy and consolation to the Man-God, a sort of paradise of delights in the midst of a world saturated with sin.

One of the great afflictions of the Word incarnate, on entering this world, is to see how *original sin makes an instrument of iniquity out of this human body,* created to be an instrument of justice.

A hideous deformity is produced in the rational being as soon as the body ceases to be subject to the soul, and a deformity more hideous still when the body enslaves the soul and forces it to put its whole intelligence and attention to work in satisfying the body's vilest desires.

Now the holy Child recognizes with sorrow that this leprosy exists, at least in germ, in all the children of Adam, and that its sores cover most of them.

Disheartened by this spectacle, how pleased He is to rest His gaze on my immaculate body, never troubled by the fever of lust! With what respect He kisses my brow, under which He sees my mind conceiving only thoughts purer than those of the angels! With what love He presses Himself to my heart, which He sees to be closed to any emotion that would not be perfectly pure!

Another source of affliction to the incarnate Word on His entrance into this world is to see how *original sin has perverted the providential role of woman.*

In God's plan, the charm and sweetness which radiate from her face were supposed to raise a man's mind towards infinite Beauty and infinite Goodness; the treasures of affection and devotion poured out from her heart were supposed to stimulate a man to deeper gratitude and more perfect service of his sovereign Benefactor and Master.

Alas, because of original concupiscence, further excited by the immodesty of fashions and the license of customs, too often the opposite result is produced. Too often the passing glimmer causes the eternal Light to be forgotten; the fine endowment becomes an occasion of ingratitude and betrayal of trust; she who should have been a help towards good becomes an accomplice of evil.

How soothing it is for the holy Child, faced with this unhappy sight, to turn His eyes on me, the ideal Woman who answers strictly to all the requirements of the divine plan; the radiant Dawn, who cannot penetrate into a place without lighting it up and making it wholesome; the gleaming white Lily, suggesting only thoughts of innocence and holiness; the Rose without thorns, charming the eyes without troubling them, softening the heart without wounding it.

And He sees that what I am for my contemporaries, I shall be in a still more perfect way for all who believe to the end of time: far from turning them away from God, I shall be a sweet allurement to draw them to Him.

I have a right, therefore, to the title of Mother most chaste because *I possess the most perfect chastity that can exist* in a mortal creature; I have a right to it further because I have *received the mission and the power of engendering this difficult virtue in others.*

Indispensable for the acquisition of any supernatural virtue, grace is doubly necessary for chastity. Here it is not enough to aid the weakness of nature, it is necessary to constrain nature's most uncontrollable impulses.

Normally you can obtain this indispensable grace only on condition that you ask for it with the proper dispositions. I make those dispositions easy for you.

Thus, you must implore it with a quite special humility; for you are asking deliverance from a malady that is very humiliating and often contracted through your own fault. Now you know well that a little child has no trouble in showing his mother the most dreadful mud stains nor in admitting that it was through his own carelessness or disobedience that he fell into the mud.

You must implore this grace, further, with an unfailing confidence, sure of being heard. That assurance is quite difficult when you are asking for a grace so often spurned. It becomes easy as soon as you turn to me: does a mother grow tired of lifting up a child who is always falling, of washing a child who is always getting dirty?

Finally, you must implore the grace of chastity with a special perseverance. You must be as persistent in calling for help as the devil is in tormenting you. Now is it any effort for a little child, is it not rather his need and his comfort, to cry after his mother from morning to night as often as he feels himself powerless or threatened?

Thus by the mere fact of being addressed to me, your prayer becomes more worthy of being heard. But how worthy it will be when it has become my prayer, when I present it as mine to my divine Son! In passing through the stem of the lily, the crude, loathsome juices of the soil are transformed into delicate perfumes. In passing through my immaculate heart, the poor request of the soul troubled or soiled by the impure spirit is permeated with an aroma that makes it worthy of the divine goodness!

Once the grace has been obtained which renders the practice of chastity possible and easy, *it remains for you to correspond to it* by detaching the senses and the heart without delay from everything that begins to disturb them: "If your eye is an occasion of sin to you, pluck it out and cast it from you!"[1]

Now this detachment becomes singularly easy for one who lives in habitual intimacy with me.

Because I am the Virgin par excellence, the Immaculate, the All-Pure, I give health to the eyes that are often fixed on my image; I give health to the memory, the imagination, the intellect that frequently meditate my greatness and my kindness; above all, I give health to the heart that strives to maintain a tender, generous love for me.

Moreover, the mere act of calling on me begets purity. If in the depths of the worst temptations you take care to raise your eyes to me and to seek refuge in my arms, my shining

[1]*Matt.* 18:9.

image will quickly dissipate the unhealthy mists and dangerous pictures that besiege your imagination or your memory.

It may happen nevertheless that the temptation persists, because the devil is resolved to more and more violent assaults on you, or because the world tries to seduce you with more and more fascinating allurements.

Thanks to my power as Queen of heaven and earth, I can offer you adequate protection against these two formidable enemies. With one look I can drive away the devil, who fears me "as an army drawn up for battle"[2]; at least I can prevent him from harassing you at too close range. It is also in my power to influence the course of events and the hearts of men, to remove from your path an unavoidable stumbling block, an over-dangerous occasion of sin.

Remember, however, that to profit from this exceptional help and protection, you must desire it, beg for it untiringly and even deserve it through a sincere devotion.

Therefore, my child, whatever may be the state of your soul, do not fail to have recourse to the Mother most chaste, to preserve or recover chastity.

Is this virtue strongly established in you? I will help you practice it in its most exacting demands. Is it still precarious or threatened? You will find in me the gentlest refuge and at the same time the safest. Is it lost, are you plunged into the pit of sinful habits? Constant recourse to my intercession is the ladder offered you by infinite Mercy to escape from that dungeon, on condition, however, that you have the desire to get out of it and that your devotion to me tends to obtain your conversion, not to lull your remorse to sleep.

[2] *Cant.* 6:3.

MOTHER EVER VIRGIN

PERPETUAL VIRGINITY OF MARY

I T is a truth of faith that I conceived and bore the Man-God without losing my virginity.

What a unique, breath-taking prodigy! but not impossible for God to accomplish. If He was able to produce the body of the first Adam with neither father nor mother, why should He not be able to produce that of the new Adam with the concurrence of a mother alone? And if He was able to make the body of Christ pass through the closed door of the upper room, why should He not be able to have it born by a similar miracle?

But for what reasons, my child, did God want the body of Christ to be *conceived virginally?*

He wanted it first of all *for Christ.* There is constant harmony between the order of grace and that of nature. According to nature a son cannot have two fathers; having already a Father who is God Himself, Christ could not have another. Moreover, it is absolutely repugnant to suppose that the Word incarnate should be subject, even simply by right, to the law of original sin; but this would have been the case if He had

had a man for father. A God, says St. Bernard, could be born only of a virgin.[1]

He wanted it *for me,* so as to point up the excellence of my divine motherhood. For as Jesus has no father according to the flesh, it is from me alone that He receives all the elements of His body, all His heredity, all His resemblance; it is on me alone that He turns His filial affection; it is I alone whom He permits to say to Him in union with the heavenly Father, "You are my true Son."

He wanted it, finally, *for all men.* The phases of Christ's bodily life are the model for the phases of your spiritual life. Now it is virginally, through the concurrence of the Holy Spirit and the Virgin, that your souls are engendered to the supernatural life. Therefore it is in the same manner that His body had to be engendered to the natural life.

Above all, every mystery of His earthly life must serve to liberate men from sin and the inclination to sin. It is not proper, therefore, that His conception call to mind the least idea of concupiscence, as would be the case if it were not virginal.

Virginal conception calls for *virginal birth.*

This is a *demand of infinite Wisdom.* As a result of original sin, it was decreed for Eve and her daughters that they should give birth in sorrow, to remind everyone that they were bringing into the world beings who were stillborn to supernatural life and "children of wrath" in the eyes of God. Now I was preserved from original sin, and the Child whom I was to bring into the world was the beloved Son of God, Author

---

[1] *Second Sermon on the Glories of the Virgin Mother,* #1; in *P. L.,* vol. 183, col. 61; in *St. Bernard's Sermons for the Seasons and Principal Festivals of the Year,* vol. 1, p. 68.

of supernatural life. Divine Wisdom owed it to Itself, therefore, to exempt me from this decree.

It is also a *demand of infinite Love.* The Word could show
me no greater honor and no greater love than to choose me,
among all, from whom to receive all that a child receives from
his mother. Is it admissible that He wanted to grant me this
supreme honor and love only at the cost of a forfeiture and a
lessening in me? No! Just as the mind is unchanged by the
bursting out of thought and the crystal by the entrance and
departure of a ray of light, so my virginity was unchanged by
the birth of Christ, eternal thought and eternal light.

As a standing proof of His unique love, Christ wants me
to be the Model of virgins, the one who draws them into the
noble paths of virginity by the sweet radiance of her example.
He wants me to the Mother of virgins, the one who merits
and obtains for them and dispenses to them those graces of
choice without which they could not walk for long in that
difficult way. He wants me to be the Queen of virgins, the
one who leads their procession in heaven, following the Lamb,
and teaches them the mysterious canticle which none but they
can learn. Hence it must be vital to Him that my virginity
be preserved intact, even at the price of the greatest miracle.

It remains for me to show you how my immaculate Heart
remained a virgin's heart even while becoming a mother's
heart and a spouse's heart.

Far from hindering mother love, virginal love conferred
on it *an increase of perfection* which made it more worthy of
a Child-God.

Thus, without taking away any of its spontaneity, virginal
love *penetrated* mother love *with reverence* and turned it into

a real adoration by showing it always, in the little body which I carried in my arms, the body of my God. The fact is that the virgin's eyes are always seeking God and perceiving Him through the most opaque veils.

Without taking away any of its tenderness, my virginal love infused into my mother love *a marvelous strength,* capable of making it sacrifice the very object of that tenderness. The virginal heart refuses nothing to God; it gives up all to Him; it immolates all to Him, as I did on Calvary.

Finally, without taking away any of its charm and sweetness, my virginal love made my mother love *purer and more disinterested,* by preserving it from the more or less conscious egoism which inclines it to relish its own emotion or to look eagerly for a response to its embrace and its caresses. For the virginal heart excludes as an indelicacy all self-seeking, even the most innocent.

Just as it was able to ally itself with a perfect motherly affection for Jesus, my virginal love knew how to ally itself with a *perfect conjugal affection* for St. Joseph.

To hide my virginal motherhood, which was not to be revealed until later, and to offer men a perfect symbol of the union of Christ with the Church, at the same time virginal and fruitful, God willed the existence of a true marriage and consequently a true conjugal love between me and St. Joseph: "Joseph, the husband of Mary."[2]

But, as we were keeping our promise to remain virgins, that conjugal love had to remain virginal.

And this is how it remained virginal. What I saw and loved in the person of St. Joseph was the child of God, the

[2] *Matt.* 1:16.

protector and friend given by God to my weakness. What I saw in the care and affection with which he surrounded me was a care and affection issued from the very heart of God and turned upon me through the agency of His servant. But are not those the characteristics of virginal love, which sees God in all things and which loves only in God and for God?

It was the same with St. Joseph's love for me. And it was just that virginal quality of our love which allowed us to live in close intimacy and show each other the most tender affection without imperiling the virginity of the senses or of the heart.

Mother ever virgin! By praying to me and honoring me under this title, Christian mothers will learn to love their children in God; that is to say, to discern, to revere, to esteem above all the supernatural being which Baptism has conferred on them and which makes them children of God and members of Christ. They will learn also to rear their children for God rather than for themselves; and if He wants to have them for Himself alone, to give them to Him generously, as I gave mine.

Christian virgins will learn to be jealously faithful to all the demands of their consecration, so as to become always better fitted for the spiritual motherhood which causes Jesus to be born in souls. For the more their love of God comes to be without division and without reserve, like mine, the more power they will have to awaken or to reawaken supernatural life, to preserve it or cause it to increase in a great number of souls, who for that reason will honor and love them in heaven as their own mother.

UNSULLIED MOTHER

MARY PRESERVED FROM ALL INCLINATION TO SIN

I AM unsullied in the sight of God and His angels because I was preserved not only from all original and personal sin, but also from *all inclination to sin.*

For what reasons, my child, did the Word incarnate decree this ultimate preservation for me?

He willed it first of all *for His own honor.* If His mercy inclines Him to take your weakness upon Himself, still His holiness demands that He be exempt from your moral lapses, not by way of privilege but by a natural right.

Now, that the flesh of Christ be preserved by a natural right from the evil heredities accumulated in the human race, there is only one means: that it be born of a flesh preserved from them by way of privilege.

Though the palm tree of Cades, to which the liturgy compares me,[1] drew its sap from putrid water, it transmitted only the purest juices to its flower and its fruit. In the same way, my immaculate flesh had its roots in a fallen race, yet communicated only an absolutely pure substance to Christ's humanity, the splendid flower born of it.

[1] *Ecclus.* 24:18; feast of the Rosary, 1st nocturn, 2nd lesson.

To look at it another way, what is the inclination to sin, what is concupiscence, if not the poisonous seed with which Satan has infected human nature and which, having issued from him, bears fruit only for him?

If I had not been preserved from the inclination to sin, Satan could say therefore to Christ, "I have got the better of You: I have debased and soiled You by debasing and soiling Your Mother." How could the Word, all knowing and all powerful, expose Himself to such an outrage, since the Mother's fall would reflect upon the Son?

But, if it is for His honor, it is *also for His consolation* that He has willed me to be exempt from all inclination to sin. In the midst of a world submerged by the muddy flood of sin, I am the islet of purity on which infinite holiness can rest His eyes with delight. In the midst of a cursed world, covered with brambles and thorns, I am the lily most pure, on which His love can bend all its affection.

As St. Grignion de Montfort says, I am "the paradise of God.... He has made a world for wayfaring man, which is that world in which we dwell; He has made one for man in his glorified state which is heaven; and He has made one for Himself, which He has called Mary."[2]

Finally, it is *through love for me* that He has willed me to be free from all inclination to sin.

From all eternity He sees that the least inclination to sin would render me unworthy of being associated with Him as Co-Redeemer; for it would not be fitting that she who is to be, with Him and through Him, the adversary of Satan and

[2] *The Secret of Mary,* translated by the Rev. A. Somers, S.M.M. (London: Burns Oates & Washbourne, 1926), p. 13.

the destroyer of his kingdom, should be dishonored (be it only for a minute) by Satan's mark.

He sees that it would render me unworthy to be associated in His reign over the angels. For that reign supposes that I be superior to them in everything, as far as moral perfection is concerned; and they have never known the inclination to sin.

He sees that it would render me unworthy of perfectly pleasing the three divine Persons, for even in germ it would create in my soul seven opaque points, seven points impermeable to the radiation of Their light; and this would prevent me from being wholly beautiful and acceptable in Their eyes.

He sees, finally, that it would render me incapable of responding perfectly to Their love, for the seven evil inclinations are like seven wild sprouts that dispute the sap of the soul with the supernatural graft of grace and charity.

Seeing in this way all the serious harm that would be done me by the inclination to sin, and having full power to make me immune to it, would He be the most loving of sons if He had not done so?

You may be sure that He did not fail! Because from all eternity the Word knows me and loves me as His Mother, He shelters me, from my very entry into existence, under the two wings of His tenderness and His omnipotence. How could the devil sow his accursed tares in a soul so jealously guarded?

To understand the great benefit of this preservation, take a minute to compare my powers with yours.

God takes no delight *in your senses;* for He sees them all prone to covet whatever pleases them without bothering about whether it is forbidden, in fact to covet more eagerly what is more strictly forbidden. By contrast, He takes a supreme delight in my senses, because His eyes, which nothing escapes, have never discovered in them the least attempt or the least desire to see, hear or touch what He forbids or deprecates.

God takes no pleasure, either, in *your imagination or your memory,* prompt to indulge in the most frivolous images with delight and with an ever increasing appetite, but incapable of dwelling on the sufferings of Jesus without quickly experiencing a great weariness, if not distaste.

By contrast, throughout my life God takes supreme pleasure in my memory and imagination; for they appear to Him as two beautiful mirrors, unsoiled by any dirt, unfogged by any steam, which register with perfect fidelity the hidden life, the public life and the suffering life of the Word incarnate.

God reproaches *your mind* with preferring the search for natural and perishable realities to the pursuit of supernatural and eternal realities, the contemplation of the creature to that of the Creator.

In mine He has the joy of contemplating the opposite disposition. For me creation is a book in which everything speaks of God: in the humble duties of my state I see His will; in every happy or unhappy event, His good pleasure; in the humblest creatures (water or fire, plant or animal), His faithful servants whom He graciously commands to serve me; and, as soon as I perceive on a human countenance a reflection of His goodness, His wisdom, His beauty, instead of lingering over this passing reflection I rise immediately to the eternal source from which it emanates.

However unruly your mind may be, *your heart* is much more so. Sensitive to the least vapors of sympathy coming to it from creatures, it remains cold before the evidences of impassioned love lavished on it by Jesus. And if sometimes it succeeds in rendering love for love to this perfect Spouse, the flame is only a flickering one, intermittent and smoky.

From my immaculate Heart, in contrast, God is overjoyed to see mounting towards Him the purest of flames, never obscured by the smoke of evil inclinations; the most ardent of flames, draining and consuming the last bit of my energy for the glory of God.

Thus, when at my last gasp the angel comes to tie the sheaf of all the thoughts my mind has produced, the sheaf of all the affections that have sprung up in my heart, the sheaf of all the sensations or emotions that have arisen in my senses, he will have to recognize that no noxious weed, no wild sprout has come to mingle with the pure wheat.

Respect and admire this ineffable purity, my child, but remember that it was given me the better to serve the cause of poor sinners like yourself.

Because I am ideally pure, I exercise such an irresistible attraction on the Holy Spirit that He hastens to whatever place I call Him. Do not fail, therefore, to cry unceasingly to me, that I may obtain for you, unceasingly, that Spirit of holiness who alone is capable of putting to rights all your powers which have been bent towards evil.

In particular, that is the meaning and the intention you are to give to the prayer which the Church puts so often upon your lips: "Pray for us sinners: Virgin most pure, who have so firm an opposition to sin, pray for us, who have so great a propensity to sin!"

LOVABLE MOTHER

MARY, BEST OF MOTHERS

I AM the most lovable of mothers, my child, first because of the *incomparable care* with which I protect and nourish your spiritual life.

To shelter Himself from the weather or to escape from Herod, the Child Jesus did not want to use His omnipotence: He trusted in my solicitude alone; and you know with what zeal I watched over Him! Now just as He entrusted to me the custody of His body, He has entrusted to me the custody of your soul; and I take no less care of this mystical member of Jesus than I took of His fleshly members.

In reality it is I who have erected around your soul the protective barrier of a Christian family and education. It is I who have fortified it with the precious shield of the faith, which shelters it from the allurements of the world. It is I who have clothed it with that "breastplate of justice"[1] against which the sting of evil inclinations is broken. For these are the work of grace, and I am the Dispenser of all graces.

[1] *Eph.* 6:14.

I have no less solicitude to nourish your spiritual life and make it increase.

You like to contemplate me in the humble home of Nazareth, nourishing the Child Jesus with the food proper to His age. That is the image of what I do for your soul, a touching picture and an accurate one. I am constantly bending over your soul, to supply it at the right time with the graces of light or charity which must nourish its supernatural life of knowledge and love. And to this end I arrange things for you: at one time a sermon, some good reading, a pious exercise or an interior inspiration which prompts you to go and draw upon the grace in the Heart of Jesus; at another time the fruitful reception of a sacrament, penance or communion, which pours the grace into your own heart.

I am the most lovable of mothers because of the *unutterable condescension* with which I accommodate myself to all your littlenesses.

Bread is too strong a food for the infant; the mother must change it into milk. That is why, after sparing no effort to procure the graces of Christ in abundance for you, I dispense them to you in a motherly way, adjusted to the weakness of your mind, your heart, your will.

An infant needs to be consoled and fondled. Observing that you quickly break away from the service of God when you find no delight in it, I do not hesitate to lavish upon you the consolations of piety as soon as you apply yourself seriously to devotion to me. After a long period of laxity you find it very hard to renew your contact with Jesus. I always respond immediately to your first call, offering myself to you as an ever accessible source of consolation and joy. Do not forget this when you grieve to find yourself in a state of dryness, whether this be a trial or a punishment. I never refuse my little one a smile. "Whosoever is a little one, let him come to me!"[2]

I am the most lovable of mothers because of the *incomparable patience* with which I endure your childish faults.

Careless, reckless child, you find yourself especially attracted to the mud that soils or the brambles that tear. But no matter how often you return to me with new stains and new hurts, you find me always eager to obtain for you the grace of light to reveal your many mud-stains, the grace of repentance to purify you immediately, leaving no trace of them.

Capricious child, from morning to evening you waste the costly bread of grace which I distribute to you with so much care. You even go so far as to develop a distaste for that indispensable food of your soul, and subbornly to reject it. Shall I let myself be repulsed by your sulkiness? No! my untiringly patient love dogs your footsteps, watching for the hour when you will be better disposed, to offer you anew the rejected grace, using every kind of ingenuity to make you accept it.

I have just as much patience to endure your incurable childish giddiness, which does not allow you to pray to me or praise me for a quarter of an hour without going through numerous distractions; your childish inconstancy, which makes you shorten or neglect the exercises in my honor on the least pretext; your childish laziness and selfishness, which incline you to lavish evidences of affection on me but to draw back before the first service or sacrifice I ask for.

[2] *Prov.* 9:4; Common of feasts of the Blessed Virgin Mary, 1st nocturn, 3rd lesson.

Finally, I am the most lovable of mothers because of the *unutterable compassion* I feel for your trials.

Some of those trials are primarily a punishment. I strive to preserve or deliver you from them, especially if the punishment is a spiritual one, a withdrawal of graces, the more formidable because you do not even suspect it.

Other trials are no more than the sad infirmities left by sin in your soul, which hardly bother you. But I, who love that poor soul incomparably more than you do, suffer to see it tormented by the fever of evil inclinations, blinded by the delusions of the world, paralyzed by the shackles of lukewarmness. And, since my compassion is as active as it is tender, I spare no effort to procure purifying and healing graces for your soul.

Other trials envisage especially the good of your soul. They are the burning cautery used by the divine Physician to open an abscess that is poisoning you; or the hard chisel by which the divine Sculptor wants to engrave His own image in you.

Do you expect me to shelter you from these painful but beneficent blows? God forbid! I am not one of those mothers more sensitive than sympathetic, who recoil in the face of a necessary treatment.

Nevertheless, I have suffered too much myself not to be moved at the suffering of your flesh or your soul, writhing under the blows of the trial. Thus, as soon as you come to pour out your pain or suffering into my motherly heart, I know how to speak words so sweet that they render you capable of carrying your cross with resignation and courage, if not with joy and love.

There, my child, is the kind of wholly lovable mother Jesus has given you! Could He make you a gift more agreeable and more heart-stirring?

Admire and praise His wisdom, which makes use of my motherly love, so evident to your heart, to give you an idea of His infinite love. Admire and praise His goodness. But in return, make it a point to thank Him and to thank me by responding to my mother love with a truly filial affection.

ADMIRABLE MOTHER

THE IMITATION OF MARY

ADMIRATION may be expressed by praise. Beyond such admiration is the kind shown by imitation.

Through veneration, my child, you offer me the homage of your mind, and through love the homage of your heart. Through imitation you offer me the homage of all your powers: your mind, which must contemplate my virtues; your heart, which must fall in love with them; your will, which must work at reproducing them.

Imitation, therefore, is the most total and perfect homage you can render me. The best fruit of love, says St. Augustine, is imitation.[1]

Moreover, when the other kinds of homage do not blossom into imitation, there is danger of superficiality or insincerity. Your failure to aim and work at imitating my virtues is undeniable proof that you have not much admiration or love for them. It is proof also that you have not much love for me. He who loves me ardently makes an effort to resemble me in everything, either because he is aware of giving me

[1] *Sermo* 304, #2; in *P. L.,* vol. 38, cols. 1395-1396.

great pleasure in that way or because all true love takes pleasure in imitating the loved one.

Besides being an *excellent means of glorifying me,* the imitation of my virtues is also an *excellent means of sanctifying yourself.*

To acquire the virtues you must first of all ask for them. Hence you must desire them, for a person does not ask sincerely for what he does not want. Now, considered in themselves, purity, humility, charity and the other virtues may appear lovable and desirable to your reason and your faith, but not to your heart and still less to your feelings. By contrast, purity and humility contemplated in me appear supremely lovable and desirable to all your faculties, and this inclines you to implore them with fervor and perseverance.

It remains for you to correspond to the grace obtained by your prayer. To know the meaning of this grace you have only to observe the example of Jesus. But often you dare not raise your guilty eyes to Him who is your God and Judge as well as your Savior; you dare not raise your sick eyes toward the Sun of justice who dazzles them with His flashing brightness.

It is no trouble for you, on the other hand, to fix your eyes constantly on me, a mere creature with a mission of pure mercy.

Besides being Mother of mercy, I am equally the faithful Virgin. I have followed Jesus step by step in all His paths; one who sets out after me, therefore, is sure of following Jesus and consequently of going in the direction of grace. I am a most pleasing copy of Christ, and at the same time a most faithful copy; one who reproduces my virtues, therefore, is sure of reproducing the virtues of Christ, the supreme Model.

Moreover, since I direct the dispensation of grace at my good pleasure, I make sure of rewarding those who strive to imitate me by granting them special lights to show them clearly what must be done or avoided and special assistance to help them surmount all obstacles. And this makes them say, "Draw us ever more, immaculate Virgin, for we run swiftly after you in the paths of virtue."

How can you put this imitation into practice?

First of all, develop the habit of *often confronting your faults with my virtues* and asking yourself questions like these: "In her relations with God would the Blessed Virgin have prayed as I am praying now, with this careless posture, this hurried recitation, this dreamy mind, this indifferent or tired heart?

"In her relations with her neighbor would she have permitted herself, as I so often do, these rash or suspicious judgments, these feelings of antipathy, jealousy, rancor, these words of detraction or mockery, these shocking or indelicate actions, these mixtures of sensuality and charity?

"In the duties of her state would she have admitted, as I do, this general negligence or at least this choosing between what pleases and what does not, these subtle calculations of self interest, or these still more subtle desires to please, to be seen, to prevail over others?

"Finally, would she have permitted her eyes, as I do mine, to rest on disturbing objects, her imagination or memory to entertain dangerous dreams or memories, her heart to nurture a suspect affection?"

This simple confrontation will unmask for you in an instant your most hidden disorders, will make you feel all their ugliness and will inspire you with an active desire to put an end to them.

After having discovered and disavowed your faults in this way, apply yourself above all *to contemplating and reproducing my virtues.*

Are you at prayer? Call to mind and imitate my attitude when I was speaking to God: my exterior attitude, respectful and recollected; my interior attitude, a constant mingling of respect and abandonment, humility and assurance, the abasements of adoration and the flights of love.

Are you assisting at Mass? Call to mind and imitate my dispositions on Calvary: let your eyes be fascinated by the wounds of Jesus; let your heart be carried away by horror of sin and love of the Savior; let your soul keep offering the gentle Lamb to the Father and offering itself with the Lamb.

You have just received Jesus in Communion. Think with what reverence and tenderness I clasped the Child Jesus in my arms and against my heart, with what fervor I gave myself entirely to Him, to thank Him for having given Himself entirely to me!

You are reading or listening to the word of God. Think with what eagerness I welcomed the least words of Jesus, with what joy I made them live again in my heart, with what fidelity I put them into practice.

You are living in a family or a community. Recall how I surrounded Jesus and Joseph with an ever wakeful solicitude and an ever active devotion, how I showed myself simple and cordial, agreeable and helpful to my neighbors at Nazareth.

You have to deal with little ones, with the lowly. Imitate my condescension and my goodness. You have to deal with the unhappy: imitate my compassion; with intruders: imitate my patience. You have to deal with wicked people, with persecutors. Close your heart to hatred and vengeance, as I did on Calvary; grant them your pardon and obtain God's pardon for them.

The duties of your state impose tedious or difficult tasks on you. Call to mind my life in Nazareth, where I had to sweep the modest house, light the fire, prepare the food, wash and mend the clothes, cultivate a dry garden; where I performed these humble, hard duties with much care, as the task prescribed by my God; with much love, as the service of my gentle Son.

Similarly, however obscure or tiresome the duties of your state may be, fufill them with the same care and the same love, encouraging yourself always by my example, so sweetly persuasive.

Finally, are you in the grip of anxiety and anguish, as I was during St. Joseph's doubt or on the way into exile or at the approach of the Passion? Despite everything, keep yourself in holy peace by casting yourself headlong into the arms of Providence, as I did.

Are you crushed by an ordeal, as I was at Calvary? Make the ordeal a sanctifying one for yourself and redemptive for your brethren by acquiescing with reverence and love, as I did, in the whole compass of the will of God, your sovereign Master and beloved Father.

Thus in any activity or any state whatsoever, it is easy for you to call to mind and imitate the interior dispositions I had in parallel activities or states.

Resolve, therefore, my child, to adopt and to cultivate perseveringly a practice so glorious for me and so profitable for your soul. That is the wise counsel given you by St. Bernard: "That you may more surely obtain the assistance of the Virgin's prayer, neglect not to walk in her footsteps."[2]

[2] *Second Sermon on the Glories of the Virgin Mother*, #17; in *P. L.*, vol. 183, col. 70; in *St. Bernard's Sermons for the Seasons and Principal Festivals of the Year*, vol. 1, p. 92.

MOTHER OF GOOD COUNSEL

MARY, TEACHER OF OUR VIRTUES

THAT he may learn to live as a man, in a rational manner, the little child needs his mother's constant instruction and counsel. That you may learn to live as a Christian, in a supernatural manner, you have no less need, my child, of being constantly guided and counseled by your heavenly Mother.

God sees, in fact, that as long as you are on earth your souls have all the inexperience and all the helplessness of a little child, and He has given me the mission of being their Teacher. That is why the liturgy puts upon my lips this invitation of Wisdom: "Whosoever is a little one, let him come to me!"[1]

Ignorant child, you have no sense of the value of things. Excited over trifles, you slight the richer gifts of your heavenly Father: faith, grace, heaven; you barter the most precious merits for a stupid conceit; and, when Mass or Communion comes to put all the treasures of Jesus at your disposal, you draw upon them only a very little and without eagerness.

[1] *Prov.* 9:4; Common of feasts of the Blessed Virgin Mary, 1st nocturn, 3rd lesson.

As *teacher of your faith* I have the mission of training you to place a just value on supernatural goods, the least of which is more precious than all the goods of this world; of training you also to discern them under the opaque veil of sacrament, duty or trial. That is why the liturgy calls me Mother of knowledge: "Mater agnitionis."[2]

Improvident child, wholly absorbed by the fleeting today, you have little concern for the eternal tomorrow; you do not know enough to fear its threats or desire its promises, forming such a vague idea of heaven and hell that it can never sharpen and stimulate your spiritual life.

As *teacher of your hope* I have the mission of detaching you little by little from earthly preoccupations, in order to make you seek, before all and at any price, the place of glory and blessedness which Jesus has prepared for you in heaven: "I am the Mother of holy hope."[3]

Self-centered child, you do not know how to discern or appreciate your heavenly Father's love; still less do you know how to respond to it.

As *teacher of your charity* I reveal to you God's fatherly affection, of which mine is a splendid reflection. I teach you to love Him with a truly filial love, more eager to serve than to enjoy, to give than to receive: "I am the Mother of fair love."[4]

Impolite child, you do not know how to observe the respect due to your Creator and Master: speaking to Him without paying attention to what you say, leaving Him for the

---

[2] *Ecclus.* 24:24 (Vulgate); Epistle of the Motherhood of the Blessed Virgin Mary.
[3] *Ibid.*
[4] *Ibid.*

first idle fancy, then coming back to Him, then leaving Him again, as if you were playing a game.

As *teacher of your religion* I train you to behave before God with great interior and exterior reverence. I urge you to thank Him every time you receive a favor from Him, or to ask His pardon every time He receives an affront from you: "I am the mother of fear."[5]

Thoughtless child, you are inclined to do whatever pleases you immediately, without being concerned whether it pleases God, your Master and Father.

As *teacher of your prudence* I lead you little by little to choose the most holy will of God as the only rule of your actions. And at the times when you must make a grave decision for yourself or others, I put you on guard against the influence of the world or of evil inclinations, which push you in the direction opposite to that adorable will. "Prudence is mine!"[6]

Child *heedless* of the rights of others, it often happens that you harm the reputation of your brethren by detraction, that you injure the authority of superiors by criticism and, still more often, that through vanity you appropriate to yourself an esteem or praise which belongs to God alone.

As *teacher of your justice* I train you to discern and respect the most exacting demands of that virtue: "Equity is mine."[7]

Faint-hearted child, you fear the least effort and the least sacrifice, so that your spiritual progress resembles the walking

[5] *Ibid.*
[6] *Prov.* 8:14 (Vulgate); Common of feasts of the Blessed Virgin Mary, 1st nocturn, 1st lesson.
[7] *Ibid.*

of a little child who stops, withdraws or turns before each new obstacle.

As *teacher of your strength* I train you to will firmly whatever God commands or counsels and to pursue it stubbornly, despite the opposition of the world and the repugnance of your own nature: "Strength is mine."[8]

Frivolous child, you are inclined to covet eagerly every pleasure you meet, without bothering about whether it is forbidden, and sometimes to covet it more eagerly, the more strictly it is forbidden.

As *teacher of your virtue of temperance* (and especially of its most difficult form, chastity) I train you to bring your senses into subjection, to cleanse your imagination, to close every avenue of your heart to dangerous or guilty affections by filling it with the great and noble love of Jesus: "I am the Mother most pure."

Yes, I make you love and desire these different virtues by the attractive example I give of each of them; I procure the means for you to acquire them surely and promptly by the superabundant graces I obtain for you. And since it is these graces that make the virtues come to life and increase in your soul, the liturgy does not hesitate to make me say that the virtues are mine and that I am their mother: "Prudence is mine.... I am the Mother of fair love...."[9]

Such is the way in which I discharge my function as teacher. Here are the *duties* that function imposes on you.

First of all you must show me the most lively *gratitude* on every occasion, considering with what condescension, what

---

[8] *Iibd.*
[9] *Ibid.; Ecclus.* 24:24 (Vulgate); Epistle of the Motherhood of the Blessed Virgin Mary.

patience and tenderness I am always bending over your soul, to teach it to walk in the difficult paths of virtue. And it goes without saying that your thanks must mount up to God. In His tender compassion for your childish weakness, He fears that an angel would not become sufficiently adjusted to all the littlenesses of your mind and your heart. That is why He has given you for teacher the wisest and most loving of mothers.

Next, you must make it as easy as possible for me to guide you as I think proper. This supposes that you will be diligent in *imploring* my assistance and counsel with conviction and fervor; for such is the normal condition imposed by God on those who want to obtain favors from on high: "Ask and you shall receive."[10] This frequent, fervent entreaty supposes in its turn that you will often place before your eyes the many childish weaknesses and needs I have just described for you. Convinced that of himself he knows nothing and can do nothing, the little child keeps crying after his mother. Imitate him.

Finally, you must *obey with docility* the directives and graces I lavish on you.

How can you know my directives? They are all summed up in one sentence of mine, reported by the gospel: "Do whatever Jesus tells you."[11] For my counsels and exhortations, my reproaches and encouragements have only this end in view: to make you fulfill promptly, joyfully, lovingly whatever Jesus commands or counsels.

And how can you discern the direction in which my grace inclines you, in order to conform your whole conduct to it?

[10] *Luke* 11:9.   [11] *John* 2:5.

You have only to meditate my example diligently and to ask yourself at a given moment how I would judge, speak and act if I were in your place. By striving to imitate me, to follow in my footsteps, you are sure to give way to the promptings of my grace and to adjust yourself to them.

To make yourself more faithful to these three duties, recall often those words of Wisdom which the liturgy ascribes to me: "Blessed are those who keep my ways. Hear instruction and be wise, and do not refuse it. Blessed is the man who hears me, and who watches daily at my gates!"[12]

[12] *Prov.* 8:32-34; Epistle of the Immaculate Conception.

MOTHER OF THE CREATOR

LOVE OF JESUS FOR MARY

I N so far as my Son is God, He is infinite Love, the unique, eternal fire from which springs every spark of true love that burns in the heart of man or angel. In so far as He is man, His filial piety towards me (as, for that matter, all His other virtues) attains such excellence that God Himself, in the actual plan of Providence, would not know how to create a more perfect piety.

How, then, my child, can you get an idea of that filial love, so inexpressible, so incomprehensible? In the first place, *by comparing it with other children's love.*

Other children cannot love their mother before they are born; and before they have the use of reason their love is only an instinctive attachment.

My Son, by His divine heart, knows and loves me from all eternity. Yes, the eyes of the Word, who sees the future as the present, rest on me with indescribable kindness and tenderness when He creates Adam and Eve, for whose tragic fall I am to make reparation through and with Jesus; when He creates the visible universe, for which I shall praise Him better than all the angels together; when He creates the heavenly spirits, over whom He will make me Queen; finally, before the dawn of the ages, when He decides to become incarnate in this human nature, which is to be born of me.

By His human heart He loves me with the purest, most conscious love from the first moment of the Incarnation. Yes, thanks to His supernatural knowledge, which permits Him to know everything, He loves me for every drop of blood I give Him in my womb; and, once born, for every caress, every attention He receives from me.

Even after the awakening of their reason, other children's love is cooled by the faults or defects of their mother and, more often still, by their own selfishness.

Jesus, on the contrary, is the Son all-loving, who lets no beat of my motherly heart pass unnoticed. And I myself am a Mother wholly lovable, in whom nothing rebuffs but everything calls forth His filial affection.

Poor mothers! They complain that they are less loved than loving. As for me, I always receive from my gentle Son a measure of love "pressed down, shaken together, running over."[1] Many times on earth I had the feeling of being submerged under a flood of love. In heaven I see myself plunged into an ocean of love, vast and deep as the heart of the Man-God.

In other children the establishment of a home and the pursuit of a separate destiny loosen the bonds of their filial love more and more.

Jesus for thirty years wanted no other home than mine; and

[1] *Luke* 6:38.

His great mission of Savior merely strengthened our intimate ties, because it pleased Him to exercise His mission first towards me and then through me.

Being Truth and Light of the world, He loves me because He sees in me the ideal disciple, eager to receive His word and faithful to keep it in my heart,[2] in order to pass it on to others.

Being the Way and Model of all virtues, He loves me because He admires in me His living copy, His perfect imitator, capable of attracting a multitude of other imitators to Him.

Being Life and Author of grace, He loves me because He see me zealous to beg for that precious grace and earn it not only for myself but for all men.

Finally, being Sovereign Priest, He loves me because He finds me always disposed to make myself a victim with Him for the glorification of God and the redemption of men.

A second means of glimpsing the love of Jesus for me is to *consider the favors He heaps upon me;* for they are so many streams sprung from that hidden source.

As a daughter of Adam I should have contracted original sin with all its fatal consequences. His filial love does not permit this. It is intolerable to Him that His beloved Mother's soul be disfigured for a single instant by the privation of grace, soiled by the inclination to evil. And in order to let me enter into existence free from all stain, He does not hesitate to suspend the inflexible law of original sin, as once He suspended the course of the Jordan to let the ark pass.

But this filial love does not stop at preserving my soul from all sin and imperfection; it fills my soul with all possible

---

[2] *Luke* 2:51.

graces. The stars shining in the firmament are less numerous and less brilliant than the perfections and graces with which He adorns my soul. It must be said further: He confers on me a measure of grace (therefore a measure of glory and beauty, of goodness and lovableness) greater than that of the angels and the saints combined. Why? Because He loves His Mother more than all His servants together.

It is also because He loves me in a unique way that He confers unique privileges on my body. Not content with immunizing it against evil inclinations, He renders it worthy of conceiving and bringing forth His own body, while yet keeping the halo of virginity. And after extinguishing its passible, mortal life, He hastens to raise it up to the blessed, immortal life.

As much as these privileges and more than them, *the functions He entrusts to me are very revealing of His love.*

On earth He reserves to me in preference to any other the honor and the joy of being Co-Redeemer of the human race: that is to say, of cooperating through and with Him in the acquisition of all pardons and all graces.

In heaven He reserves to me the honor and the joy of being the universal Mediatrix: that is to say, of cooperating through Him and with Him in the dispensation of all graces, in order that they may be distributed to you in a truly maternal fashion. But, since transmitting graces means transmitting life, Jesus reserves to me by that very fact the honor and the joy of being the Mother, the true Mother of all the redeemed, the only one who has the power to love them with a really maternal love, the only one who has the right to be loved by them with a really filial love!

Observe how it is in reality: with what trusting affection the clear eyes of the newly baptized contemplate the image of His heavenly Mother; with what cheerfulness the consecrated virgins renounce everything to put themselves at my service; with what childlike simplicity the greatest geniuses, like St. Bernard, St. Thomas, St. Bonaventure, seek refuge in my arms. And in paradise see with what fondness the apostles and the martyrs, the confessors and the virgins look upon the motherly love and care with which I surrounded their earthly life, judging that all eternity is not too long for thanking me!

Now by whom are they moved, those on earth and those in heaven, if not by the grace or the prompting of my Son, who, not content with loving me Himself, wants to make me loved by all His members!

Finally as a supreme testimony of His love Jesus associates me in His universal reign by giving me jurisdiction and power over all creatures: over men (individuals, families, nations), to assist and defend them; over devils, to prevent them from harming you; over angels, to make them my messengers and servants. And it is a real joy to Him to see these blessed spirits gravitate around my queenly throne, always ready to receive my orders, always occupied in singing my praises.

Call to mind often, my child, this filial piety of Jesus, in order to understand and admire it better, and also to rejoice and congratulate me on being so perfectly loved.

Then, draw it into your heart by entreating Jesus at each Communion to give you an ever larger share of His affection for me.

MOTHER OF THE SAVIOR

LOVE OF MARY FOR JESUS

FROM the first moment of the Incarnation, my child, the same Holy Spirit who conferred on my body the power to conceive the body of Jesus, *conferred on my heart a maternal love* whose breadth the angels themselves could not measure and whose depth they could not sound.

This love had to be worthy, in so far as possible, of the heavenly Father's love for Jesus, our common Son. It had to be worthy of the Person of the Word, since love in the last analysis is directed to a person. It had to be worthy of the power and goodness of the Holy Spirit, who Himself without intermediary stirred it up in my heart.

Moreover, this love was able to come into play from the first instant; for unlike other mothers I knew clearly the One who was building His body, cell by cell, in my womb: the new Head of humanity, the Savior of the world, the Word incarnate!

And it was able to be exercised in all its fulness; for it did not have to be shared with any other love, since my heart was virginal, nor to conflict with any selfish inclination, since my heart was immaculate.

After the birth of Jesus the same causes which act on the heart of mothers kept heightening whatever natural affection there was in my mother love; and the uninterrupted growth of my fulness of grace kept fanning its purely supernatural flame.

The love of mothers *is heightened by the contemplation of their child's beauty.*

Who can express my rapture when, after nine months of waiting, I was able to contemplate the most beautiful of the sons of men[1] and look full in His face whenever I wished! Others marveled at His resemblance to me. I dissolved in love, discerning in Him the most faithful reflection of the infinite beauty and lovableness of God.

My love increased still more when it was given me to perceive the beauty of His soul beyond the radiant veil of the flesh. At the sight of a soul in the state of grace, great saints have gone into ecstasy. But what is the beauty of the purest soul compared to the beauty of that Soul, adorned with all the perfections of nature and of grace?

Finally when I glimpsed, beyond the soul itself, the splendor of the Word surrounding it with His own glory, my mother love, without losing any of its tenderness, was changed into a profound adoration. To love their son to the point of adoration would be a crime for other mothers. For me it was the first of duties, for my Son was truly my sovereign Good.

The love of mothers *is heightened by reason of the attentions and the devotion* they lavish on their little one.

[1] *Psalm* 44:3.

And in fact my love for Jesus increased each time I had to take Him in my arms, dress Him, prepare His food, make His clothes, guide His first steps. Was He not the flesh of my flesh and, at the same time, Goodness Itself!

But I joined to that love of compassion or affection, common to all mothers, a love of gratitude which no other can feel. For beyond the indigence and weakness of the Newborn I discerned the supremely lovable condescension of my God, who had willed to make Himself poor and weak for love of me.

"O my sovereign Good," I said to Him then, "You know well that my love finds more pleasure and profit in giving than in receiving. How good You are, then, to have put Yourself into a state which permits me to render You these continual services a little one expects from his mother!"

The love of mothers *is heightened as soon as they see their child pay them some return.*

By that fact you may judge how I loved Jesus for all the signs of gratitude and filial affection He lavished on me; and He needed no visible signs, so transparent were our two souls to each other!

Imagine how I loved Him for His childish duties, performed with so much attention and zeal; and later, for His hard work as an artisan by which He earned His bread and mine in the sweat of His brow.

Imagine how I loved Him for the revelation He made to me of God and divine things. Was not my heart incomparably more loving and discerning than that of the disciples of Emmaus, warmed by His discourse?

Imagine how I loved Him for the prayers He said with me and for my intention. Truly I had the impression then of abiding in the shadow of the Almighty and of taking refuge under His wings,[2] as the Psalmist says.

Finally, the love of mothers *is heightened at the sight of the sufferings* that threaten or afflict their child.

I knew that Jesus was to be a victim for all men, and I had received the mission of nourishing Him and keeping Him for the day of His sacrifice. Hence it was not only on the way into exile, enfolding Him in my arms, that I was moved by the fate of that gentle Lamb. Would not my love be doubled by wrapping in swaddling clothes those tender limbs which I saw in advance fastened to the cross with huge nails? by hearing the beat against my heart of that childish heart which would one day be pierced by the lance and which even then was grief-stricken at the sight of the endless flood of outrages cast up by men against His beloved Father?

Above all, how could I help being overwhelmed by love for that divine Son when I had to travel with Him each one of those five abysses of disgrace and suffering which are the five sorrowful mysteries? Then my love made me feel all the interior and exterior sufferings of Jesus as if they were my own. But in return this sword of sorrow, in piercing my heart through, drew from it the last drop of love it could possibly give to Jesus: love of compassion for that tender Son, who had never had so much to suffer; love of gratitude and kindness for my gentle Savior, who had never revealed Himself more loving or more lovable than at that hour when

[2] *Psalm* 90:1,4.

He was paying the price of my redemption and that of all men.

There, my child, is a faint conception of what my love for Jesus was on earth. But as soon as I entered heaven, the face-to-face contemplation of His twofold beauty, divine and human, conferred on that love *an immeasurable increase.*

The angels and the saints, enraptured, see that love emitted from my heart like a pure flame (for in heaven everything is visible and transparent), and they never tire of offering it to their beloved King to make up for the insufficiency of their own love. Do not fail to make the same offering frequently, especially during your thanksgiving, when you grieve at loving so little the One who loves you so much! Do not fail, either, to ask of me often a greater love for Jesus; for no one is more desirous than I of obtaining for you that precious grace above all others.

VIRGIN MOST PRUDENT

MARY, TEACHER OF OUR PRUDENCE

"PRUDENCE is mine, counsel is mine."[1] These words ascribed to me by the liturgy remind you, my child, that I have received from God the mission and the power of initiating into Christian prudence those who are zealous to implore my aid and imitate my example.

First of all I form you to Christian prudence by teaching you to *discern the manifold dangers* of a supernatural order which lie in wait for you at every step.

While you are very careful of your temporal possessions, an incurable carelessness exposes you to leaving *your spiritual substance* of graces and merits unproductive or to *squandering it heedlessly.*

That your supernatural riches may increase, I inspire in you a great zeal to draw upon the stream of graces which Jesus causes to flow before you during every Mass, every Communion, every pious exercise.

In the same way I incite you to fulfill the various duties of your state and to sustain your various trials for God and in a manner worthy of God; for without fail He allots a mag-

[1] *Prov.* 8:14; Common of feasts of the Blessed Virgin Mary, 1st nocturn, 1st lesson.

nificent reward to everything done for Him. What a misfortune and what a shame it would be if, for lack of willingness to make a little effort, you were to deprive yourself of that reward, more precious than all the goods of this world put together! What a misfortune and what folly it would be for you to exchange that reward for a stupid conceit!

While you are very careful not to offend relatives, friends or benefactors, you *take no care and go to no trouble to avoid what displeases God,* your heavenly Father, your chief Friend and Benefactor.

I maintain in you the horror of grave sin by showing you in it the tormentor of Jesus during the Passion. Away with that pride or that envy, for they are nothing less than the slaps or the spittle that humiliated the soul of Jesus! Away with those impure pleasures, for it is they that bruised, tore and crucified His innocent flesh!

I maintain in you the horror of venial sin by reminding you that it grieves the Holy Spirit, the sweet guest of your soul. Away with those lies and those self-conceited kindnesses (no less lying) which afflict the Spirit of truth present in you! Away with those suspect thoughts, those disturbed feelings which afflict the Spirit of purity! Away with that back-biting, those mockeries, those little ill-natured remarks which oppose the Spirit of charity!

I go even so far as to inspire in you a horror of every imperfect disposition, liable to hinder the reign of Christ in your soul: a horror of dissipation and levity, which prevent you from hearing the ever discreet knocks of that divine Friend: "Behold, I stand at the door and knock";[2] a horror

---

[2] *Apoc.* 3:20.

of spiritual carelessness and laxity, which do not prevent you from hearing but deter you from going to open the door to Him; a horror of all those vain, perishable attachments which do indeed let Him enter into your soul but contend with Him for the best of your thoughts, your affections, your concerns.

Whereas you are very careful to procure *sufficient, healthful food* for your body, you have no similar concern for your soul.

You look on the various exercises designed to nourish your spiritual life—sermons, spiritual reading, meditation—as a painful drudgery from which you would gladly escape. I make you value them, desire them, seek them as a precious food which you must take to yourself even at the price of the greatest sacrifices.

On the other hand you hardly take the trouble to find out when a certain spectacle or reading or company is apt to poison your spiritual life. I arouse you to be as distrustful of them as you are of poisonous fruit or spoiled food.

In the second place I form you to Christian prudence by teaching you to unmask and despise *the illusion of false happiness*.

Like a royal infant left indifferent by his kingdom but enchanted by a rattle, you experience neither desire nor love for the place of glory and happiness Jesus is reserving for you in heaven, whereas you place your happiness in the goods here below: health and beauty, knowledge and culture, riches, honor, power.

To detach your heart from those false beatitudes, I show you first of all that they are *fleeting*: that they are like those wild flowers which hold themselves proudly on their stems and attract all eyes, but are withered and dried up by the sun in a few days, if the scythe has not already cut them down in their first bloom.

Will you say that new flowers can spring up on the dust of the flowers that have disappeared? I remind you that a day will come when you yourself will no longer be able to enjoy them: even before death separates you from them, your weakened senses will no longer be able to perceive their color or their perfume, and your enfeebled mind will lose even the memory of them.

Hence why not repeat with the Apostle, "Let us not look at the things that are seen, but at the things that are not seen. For the things that are seen are temporal, but the things that are not seen are eternal."[3]

Then I show you that all these blessings here below are as *deceptive* as they are fleeting.

They are deceptive because, once despoiled of the false appearance with which the imagination had clothed them, they no longer answer your expectations. They are deceiving, above all, because nothing created, nothing finite, nothing perishable can satisfy fully the hunger of a soul made for the uncreated, the infinite, the eternal. As St. John of the Cross rightly says, "All creatures are crumbs that have fallen from the table of God . . . and crumbs serve to whet the appetite rather than to satisfy hunger."[4]

[3] *2 Cor.* 4:18.
[4] *Ascent of Mount Carmel,* book 1, ch. 6; translated by E. Allison Peers in *The Complete Works of St. John of the Cross* (Westminster, Md.: The Newman Bookshop, 1946), vol. 1, p. 35.

To detach you still more effectively from these supposed blessings, I show you that they are *debasing*.

It is only too clear that an intelligent, free soul cannot help debasing and degrading itself when it seeks its happiness in carnal, animal enjoyments. But its degradation is no less real, even though less shocking, if it seeks its happiness in the noblest goods of this world: knowledge, glory, power, love. For to put one's supreme good in a creature when one is made for God is to condemn oneself to an immeasurable fall, as immeasurable as the distance between God and creature.

For these various reasons I cause you to adhere with all your soul to those supreme principles of Christian prudence formulated by the Holy Spirit in these terms: "The world with its lust is passing away, but he who does the will of God abides forever.[5] . . . Jesus Christ is the same, yesterday and today, yes, and forever.[6] . . . I count all things as dung that I may gain Christ."[7]

Finally, I form you to Christian prudence by revealing to you the *true means* of reaching that supreme objective and by unmasking for you the *illusory means*.

The true means is to seek in whatever you say and do, not what pleases men, not what pleases yourself, but what pleases God: "Seek first the kingdom of God and His justice, and all these things shall be given you besides."[8]

On the contrary, to read and meditate constantly the teachings of Christ on this kingdom, to make them the object of one's admiration and love, yet fail to translate them into

[5] *1 John* 2:17.
[6] *Heb.* 13:8.
[7] *Phil.* 3:8.
[8] *Matt.* 6:33.

action, would be a dangerously illusory means: "For it is not they who hear the Law that are just in the sight of God; but it is they who follow the Law that will be justified.[9] ... 'Not everyone who says to Me, "Lord, Lord," shall enter the kingdom of heaven; but he who does the will of My Father in heaven shall enter the kingdom of heaven.'[10] ... 'He who has My commandments and keeps them, he it is who loves me.' "[11]

There, my child, are the lessons of prudence which I cause to re-echo in the ear of those who cultivate devotion to me. Be eager to hear them from my mouth: they will appear more persuasive to you. Be eager to contemplate them perfectly lived in my various mysteries: they will appear more lovable to you. Finally, as soon as you take the trouble to conform your conduct to these lessons of prudence, be sure to implore my aid, recalling those words which the liturgy puts upon my lips: "In me is all grace of the way and of the truth, in me is all hope of life and of virtue."[12]

[9] *Rom.* 2:13.
[10] *Matt.* 7:21.
[11] *John* 14:21.
[12] *Ecclus.* 24:25 (Vulgate); Epistle of the Motherhood of the Blessed Virgin Mary.

VENERABLE VIRGIN

MEANS OF INCREASING OUR LOVE FOR MARY

T HE first evidence of veneration a mother expects from her child, the one that she prefers to any other and that no other can make up for, is a real filial love.

But, for your filial love to live up to my expectation, it is not enough, my child, that is produce some intermittent, fleeting acts, some isolated, short-lived flowers. The affection must be rooted in all your faculties: imagination and memory, intelligence, heart and will. It must drain the best of their energies and transform them into a magnificent, perfumed garden in which I shall delight to recognize all the varieties of holy love.

Such is the ideal to be desired, for, as the liturgy tells you, "I love those who love me."[1] Learn, therefore, by what means you can arouse in your heart an ever growing love for your heavenly Mother.

The first means, the most efficacious and perhaps the most neglected, is to *ask Jesus for the grace of that love* by prayer:

[1] *Prov.* 8:17; Common of feasts of the Blessed Virgin Mary, 1st nocturn, 1st lesson.

humble prayer, for you are quite unworthy of such a favor; ardent prayer, for it is a very precious gift; trusting prayer, for my divine Son has no greater desire than to grant you this gift.

A second means will be to *recall frequently the favors I have heaped upon you*. Truly nothing is so provocative of love as the feeling of being loved; and love makes itself known only through favors.

Accustom yourself, therefore, to seeing in me the sweet Guardian of your soul, always intent on protecting you against your childish imprudence, or removing a stumbling-block, or driving off a devil who is harassing you at too close range; in a word, ever intent on surrounding your soul with watchful solicitude, as the bird shelters its flock under its wings.

Accustom yourself also to seeing in me the tender Nurse of your soul, always bent over it to offer, at just the right time, the grace necessary to the growth or vitality of its supernatural being.

Accustom yourself, finally, to seeing in me the patient Governess of your soul, having received the mission of initiating it into the practice of all the virtues and of training it in that practice, through example and grace.

If you consider, moreover, that I am discharging this three-fold office of Guardian, Nurse and Governess not simply as a conscientious employee but as the fondest of mothers— that is to say, with a solicitude which foresees your least needs, a watchfulness concerned with your least perils, a condescension which adjusts itself to all your littleness, a patience never tiring of your defects or whims, a compassion bewailing your most deserved ordeals, never imposing a cross too heavy

or a pace too swift, not even refusing you those tangible consolations so indispensable to a little one—yes, if you often
put before your eyes these various aspects of my mother love,
you will not find it excessive to cry out your gratitude and love
to me a hundred times in succession, through the Hail Marys
of the rosary!

Love is heightened by the remembrance of favors, but
still more *by the remembrance of sacrifices made willingly
for us.*

Now, make no mistake, while it is a joy to me in heaven
to dispense pardon and grace to you, I had to acquire that
pardon and that grace for you on earth at a very dear price.
For the carrying of my spiritual children made my life a cross
and a martyrdom, and their birth cost me the indescribable
agony of Calvary!

Taught by the Holy Spirit, therefore, when He invites you
not to forget the groanings of your Mother,[2] you should love
to contemplate me in this office of Co-Redeemer, this mystery
of my spiritual motherhood, resigning myself to all that happens. My gentle Son, whom I love incomparably more than
myself, is plunged successively into the five depths of the
agony, the scourging, the crowning with thorns, the carrying
of the cross, the crucifixion, to let you climb up out of the
abyss in which Satan holds you chained. His beautiful face is
covered with dirt and blood, with blows and spittle, that the
brand of shame imprinted on your face by sin may be removed.
His precious blood gushes from all His wounds, and the lance
takes the last drop, that your soul may be washed clean of its

[2] *Ecclus.* 7:29.

seemingly indelible stain. Finally, He delivers Himself to death to merit life eternal for you! To all this I resign myself.

Persevere in the contemplation of this mystery of sorrow and devotedness and, however hard or cold your heart may be, it will not take long to soften, to dilate, to shatter its stony enclosure. Then you will be ashamed of having loved Her so little who has loved you so much; you will beg the saints who have loved me most to give you a share of their love; and, finding it intolerable to have nothing to offer me in return but fond words or pious affections, you will make use of everything to show me a love like mine, pure, strong, generous, more eager to give than to receive!

Love *is heightened by declaring itself and being poured out* in intimate conversations.

Arrange for yourself every day, therefore, a certain number of rendezvous with the dear Mother of your soul: Angelus, rosary, litany, prayers before and after the principal exercises. Only go to them as to a feast instead of regarding them (as sometimes happens) as a painful drudgery. And once you are at my feet, tell me with childlike candor and reliance your joys and your sorrows, your hopes and your fears, your distress, your misery, your sins.

Although self-concerned, these confidences cannot help binding us together more intimately; for I am a Mother so lovable and so loving that no one can converse with me without feeling compelled to love me.

Nevertheless your heart will want to tell me your filial love again and again, very expressly. Thus during the joyful mysteries of the rosary you will love me with a love of delight, as the Mother of God adorned with all the virtues and all the privileges. During the sorrowful mysteries you will love me with a love of compassion and gratitude, as the true Mother who has given you birth into supernatural life at the price of a cruel martyrdom. During the glorious mysteries you will love me with a love of admiration and good will, rejoicing at the knowledge that I am so great and so happy, desiring that all men honor, love and serve me!

Aside from these regular conversations you will keep thinking all day long how you may fan the flame of your filial love, whether it be by casting a glance at my image, which for what purpose you should always have within sight; or by pronouncing my blessed name; or by breathing fervent ejaculations to me: for example, in success, "Cause of our joy"; in trials, "Comforter of the afflicted"; in sickness, "Health of the sick"; in indecision, "Mother of good counsel"; in temptation, "Virgin most pure." For all these things will dispose you to love me by reminding you that I am the clement, the compassionate, the sweet Virgin Mary.

Still more than in expressing itself, *love is heightened by exerting itself* in service and sacrifice.

Do you want to acquire great love for me swiftly? Make this promise to me every day: "O sweet Mother, to please you today I am going to control and correct my habits of falsehood, frivolous looks, back-biting. To please you I am going to say with perfect care the prayer which I ordinarily say so carelessly, perform with perfect care the duty which I ordinarily fulfill with such negligence. To please you I am going to endure without complaint and even with a smile this discomfort or that setback. To please you I am going to spare no effort to improve the exercises in your honor. To please you I am going to use every means to make you known and loved by a great number of souls."

Such, my child, are the principal means of making my love flourish in your soul, of transforming your soul into a garden of roses, which I shall contemplate with delight!

Form a resolution, then, to use all these means in succession with courage and perseverance, making your own the program of St. John Berchmans: "I will give myself no rest as long as I have not acquired a very great love for the Blessed Virgin, the sweet Mother of my soul."[3]

[3] *Documenta Vitae Spiritualis* (Turin: Marietti), p. 58.

VIRGIN WORTHY OF ALL PRAISE

THE "HAIL MARY"

T HROUGH the voice of St. John Damascene the Christians of the East proclaim that "neither human tongue nor angelic mind is able worthily to praise the Virgin."[1] And through the voice of St. Bernard those of the West echo this sentiment with the cry, "What tongue, whether angelic or human, can worthily eulogize this Virgin Mother!"[2]

That is why the Holy Spirit has taken care Himself to dictate *a eulogy worthy of my inexpressible greatness,* the "Hail Mary." As it will be easier for you to repeat it to me with all your heart if you understand it better, I am going to uncover for you, my child, some of the riches the Holy Spirit has enclosed in it.

Full of Grace

Contemplating *my soul itself,* the angels admires in it a fulness of habitual grace. Whereas other souls in consequence

---

[1] *First Sermon on the Assumption,* # 2; in *Patrologia Graeca* (Paris: J.-P. Migne), vol. 96, col. 700; translated by Mary H. Allies in *St. John Damascene on Holy Images, followed by Three Sermons on the Assumption* (London: Thomas Baker, 1898), p. 148.

[2] *Fourth Sermon for the Feast of the Assumption,* #5; in *P. L.,* vol. 183, col. 428; in *St. Bernard's Sermons for the Seasons and Principal Festivals of the Year,* vol. 3, p. 253.

of original sin remain deprived of the beauty and life of grace until Baptism, there is not a single instant of my existence when the angel does not see me radiant with that life and resplendent with that beauty.

And whereas in other souls there is very often a disparity between the measure of grace they ought to have and what they have in fact, the angel can see no shortcoming in me: of all the graces it was possible for me to acquire by way of merit or of prayer, not one did I allow to be lost.

Contemplating *my various faculties,* mind, heart, and will, the angel sees in them no activity or tendency that is not wholly subject to the reign of the Holy Spirit. The fact is that there exists in me not the least root of those seven capital sins which, in you, set up steady opposition to the seven virtues: "The flesh lusts against the spirit, and the spirit against the flesh."[3]

Finally, contemplating *my immaculate body,* he perceives that all its dispositions, tendencies and habits have been so well controlled by the soul, according to the demands of grace, that the body is truly worthy to be a dwelling for the Son of God, as the liturgy says.[4]

The Lord Is with Thee

From the first moment of my conception *the Trinity* is in me in a unique manner, to communicate to me a fulness of graces and virtues greater than that destined for the angels and saints together.

The Trinity is in the essence of my soul to quicken it with Its own life; in my mind to enlighten it with knowledge more

[3] *Gal.* 5:17.
[4] Collect of the *Salve Regina.*

penetrating than that of the cherubim; in my heart to enflame it with a love more ardent than that of the seraphim; in my will to invest it with justice more indefectible than that of the thrones; in my memory and my imagination to fill them with visions purer than those of the angels; in my senses and all my members to make them the perfectly docile instruments of Its grace.

But the Incarnation ties me to each of the three Persons in a still closer union.

The Father is with me as with His privileged daughter. Did He not choose me before the dawn of the ages to be the first of His adopted children, the one whom He would use to adopt the others, the one to whom He reserves a share of His love and His inheritance greater than that of all the others together?

The Son is with me as with His beloved Mother. And I have already told you (Mother of the Creator, Mother of the Savior) what bonds unite us to each other.

The Holy Spirit is with me as with His Spouse, wholly lovable and loved, through whom He causes the elect to be born into supernatural life; but through whom, first of all, He causes the Head of all the elect to be born into natural life. Thus the billions of stars twinkling in the sky are but a pale image of the perfections with which He is pleased to adorn my soul.

Blessed Art Thou amongst Women

Among all virgins I am the only one who has ruled out not only all division between God and the creature but even the very possibility of such division.

Among all mothers I am the only one who was able to conceive solely by the power of the Holy Spirit, give birth without trouble or sorrow, and thus put on my brow the two glorious crowns of virginity and motherhood. I am the only one who has for her son God's own Son, and thus the only one who can give the Word incarnate a real maternal love and receive from Him a real filial love. Finally, I am the only one chosen to be the spiritual Mother of all men; and you may see in heaven how the countless multitude of the elect, of every tongue, nation and race, crowd around my throne to proclaim their gratitude and their filial affection.

And Blessed Is the Fruit of Thy Womb, Jesus

The praise that most delights a mother's heart is that bestowed on her child. You know that the whole effort of the Church militant, still journeying in the obscurity of faith, is to praise my divine Son and cause Him to be praised. Learn how I see Him blessed, in the light of heaven, by the Church triumphant.

With unspeakable joy I see *all the elect,* patriarchs and prophets, apostles and martyrs, confessors and virgins, uniting their voices in a magnificent chorus to sing Him this canticle of ardent gratitude: "You have redeemed us for God with Your blood, out of every tribe and tongue and people and nation, and have made them for our God a kingdom and priests.[5] We were stained with a hideous stain, and by Your blood You have cleansed us.[6] We were captives of Satan, of sin and of lusts; and by Your blood You have delivered us.[7]

[5] *Apoc.* 5:9-10.
[6] *Heb.* 9:14.
[7] *Col.* 1:13.

We were enemies of God, and by Your blood You have reconciled us with Him."[8]

Beyond the saints I see *the nine choirs of angels* sending up to my Son a still more sublime symphony of praise and benediction. They bless Him as the perfect mirror of the divine perfections "into which they desire to look;"[9] as the supreme Mediator of worship through whom they must pass to render God a homage worthy of Him: "through whom the angels praise";[10] finally, as their King and their God whom they have a mandate to serve and adore: "I heard a voice of many angels round about the throne . . . saying with a loud voice, 'Worthy is the Lamb who was slain to receive power and divinity and wisdom and strength and honor and glory and blessing!' "[11] What other mother has had a son the object of such a blessing!

And yet I see descending upon this dear Son a blessing infinitely higher, *that of the three divine Persons,* for whom to bless is to communicate a good.

I see the Word communicate to Him His own subsistence and thus confer on His human nature an infinite dignity and on all His actions an infinite value.

I see the Father recognize Him as His own Son, the object of all His love; establish Him as Pontiff of angels and men for eternity; invest Him with His royalty, His magistracy, His omnipotence in heaven and on earth.

Finally, I see the Holy Spirit communicate to Him all the fulness of knowledge and holiness, glory and beatitude that it is possible for a created being to receive.

---

[8] *Rom.* 5:10.
[9] *1 Pet.* 1:12.
[10] Common preface.
[11] *Apoc.* 5:11-12.

I am truly worthy of all praise, therefore, because I have a Son who is beyond all the praise of men and angels, and who is worthily praised by God alone.

For your part, my child, knowing that the "Hail Mary" expresses for me the admiration of the saints through the words of Elizabeth and the admiration of the angels through the words of Gabriel, you will be convinced that it is the praise I prefer to any other, and you will not grow tired of addressing it to me and putting your whole soul into it.

POWERFUL VIRGIN

POWER OF MARY'S INTERCESSION

I AM proclaimed powerful Virgin, my child, because I enjoy unlimited influence with God, which disposes Him to place His omnipotence at the service of my least desires.

Listen first to what the saints say of the unlimited power of my intercession.

St. Germanus of Constantinople: "O Mother of God, our intellect cannot conceive the power of your intercession![1] ... You have a power equal to your will!"[2] St. Bernard: "Mary always finds what she seeks and can never suffer a disappointment."[3] St. Bernardine of Siena: "Mary dispenses to whom she will, when she will, as she will, as much as she will, the gifts, the virtues and the graces of the Holy Spirit!"[4] St. Grignion de Montfort: "The will of the Most High ... is that heaven, earth and hell bend, with good will

[1] *Sermo in S. Mariae Zonam;* in *P. G.,* vol. 98, col. 381.

[2] *In Ingressum Sanctissimae Deiparae Sermo;* in *P. G.,* vol. 98, col. 320.

[3] *Sermon for the Feast of the Nativity of the Blessed Virgin Mary,* #8; in *P. L.,* vol. 183, col. 442; in *St. Bernard's Sermons for the Seasons and Principal Festivals of the Year,* vol. 3, p. 289.

[4] *Sermo* 5; in *Opera Omnia,* vol. 4, p. 93.

or bad will, to the commandments of the humble Mary."[5] St. Alphonsus de Liguori: "The Son is omnipotent by nature, the Mother is omnipotent by grace."[6]

In His desire to convince you of the complete power of my influence, God has been pleased to reinforce the testimony of the Doctors by *a testimony still more cogent, that of miracles.* It is a fact that numerous indisputable marvels, performed throughout the ages, show you that I have all power over material elements. How many times my intercession has obtained the arrest of a plague, fire or flood, preservation from an unavoidable accident, a multiplication of grain!

Miracles show you that I have all power over living beings. Do not the "ex-votos" covering the walls of my shrines attest that I can obtain the cure of any sickness or infirmity, even the most incurable? Witness the 4,400 cures registered at Lourdes from 1860 to 1914.[7]

Miracles show you that I have all power over the world of souls, whether to carry them to the highest peaks of perfection or to recover them from the depths of sin or faithlessness. The conversion of the Jew Alphonse Ratisbonne, effected before my image, instantaneously and without any preparation, is but one example of the innumerable conversions, less striking but no less marvelous, only a few of which

[5] *Treatise on the True Devotion to the Blessed Virgin Mary,* translated by the Rev. Frederick William Faber (Bay Shore, N.Y.: Montfort Fathers, 1941), #28, p. 23.

[6] *True Spouse of Christ,* translated by the Very Rev. Dr. Callan (New York: Benziger Brothers, 1913), ch. 21, #3, p. 398.

[7] Georges Bertrin, *Lourdes: A History of Its Apparitions and Cures,* translated by Mrs. Philip Gibbs (New York: Benziger Brothers, 1908). The reference here is to the appendix of a later French edition, *Histoire Critique des Événements de Lourdes.*

are mentioned in the annals of the miraculous medal, of Notre-Dame des Victoires, of Notre-Dame de Lourdes and of my other shrines.

Finally, miracles show you that I have power even over the world of spirits, angelic or diabolical. In various apparitions, for example at the Rue de Bac and at Fatima, the good angels have shown that they were my servants, active as well as respectful. And the power of my name alone against diabolical obsessions or possessions attests that I am more terrible to the spirits of darkness than an army drawn up for battle.

This extensive power comes from the fact that God is always disposed to listen to my least requests and to fulfill my least desires. But why does the Most High thus place His omnipotence, in a way, at my disposal and my service?

He owes it first of all *to His infinite wisdom,* which does not entrust anyone with a mission or a mandate without at the same time giving the means of carrying out the mission properly.

In making me the Mother of men God gives me the mission of sympathizing with all their misfortunes and coming to their aid with motherly affection and care. Therefore He must give me the power to help them all. If He did not, I should be the most unhappy and desperate of all mothers!

In the same way, by appointing me universal Mediatrix, God gives me the mandate of imploring all the graces of pardon or sanctification necessary for the various members of the mystical body. But this would be a vain mandate and a mockery if it were not accompanied by an influence capable of obtaining all these things, such as the liturgy ascribes to me: "Bona cuncta posce."[8]

[8] Hymn *Ave Maris Stella.*

God owes it further *to His infinite mercy,* which has made it a law for Him to hear every humble, trusting prayer.

No supplication could be humbler than that which I address to Him for sinners; for no one has so much light to see how great is the One whom I implore, how precious is the favor I beg, and how unworthy are those for whom I ask it.

No supplication could be more trusting, for I address myself to the most loving and grateful of all sons. If He could not resist the pleadings of a poor pagan woman asking Him to free her daughter's body from a devil, how could He reject the pleading of His own Mother, begging Him to deliver the souls of her children?

He owes it to His infinite love, for which it is a joy and a need to give pleasure to those who are the object of its affection.

Each one of the three divine Persons loves me with a special love which He cannot have for the other elect. The Father loves me as His privileged Daughter, whom He has chosen before the dawn of the ages to be His sole collaborator in the supreme work of the Incarnation. The Son cherishes me as His true Mother, lavishing on me a filial love and gratitude such that God Himself could not create any more perfect. The Holy Spirit cherishes me as His Spouse, wholly lovable and wholly loving, through whom He causes all the elect to be born into the life of grace and glory.

Loving me with such a love, the three Persons must be disposed to welcome my least requests.

Finally, *God owes it to His infinite justice* to place His omnipotence at my disposal. In His sovereign justice God assigns to the elect an influence proportioned to their merit.

Because on earth I refused God no service or sacrifice, God makes it His joy in heaven to refuse nothing to me. Because I hungered and thirsted to seek God's greatest glory in all things throughout my earthly pilgrimage, God is eager to glorify me before all the angels by placing His omnipotence at my disposal.

In His sovereign justice God will not ignore any right. But have I not a right of co-ownership, purchased at a great price, over all the graces I ask for my unhappy or guilty children? Through my "com-passion" have I not merited with a merit of equity all that Jesus through His Passion was meriting with a merit of justice?[9]

That, my child, is how I am "suppliant Omnipotence." And my motherly heart feels compelled to put this omnipotence at the service of each of my children. But as a general rule my heart cannot do this without them and in spite of them. In order to benefit from my motherly assistance and protection, you must appreciate it, desire it, implore it.

You should reproach yourself bitterly, therefore, with having rejected or ignored my offers of service many times, thus leaving your soul and the souls of your brethren alone at grips with the worst perils or trials, when you could so easily have assured them of my all-powerful protection. Do not fail henceforth to confide all your troubles in me, whether they be temporal or spiritual, whether they be those that afflict you now or those (incomparably more formidable) that await you at the hour of your death: "Nunc et in hora mortis nostrae!"

---

[9] Pius X, *Ad diem illum.*

CLEMENT VIRGIN

MARY, MOTHER OF MERCY

PRIESTS and people, saints and sinners are of one mind in seeing me as Mother of clemency, Mother of mercy. And the Church herself agrees with them when she calls me in her liturgy "Dulcis parens clementiae, Mater misericordiae!"

Strictly speaking, clemency denotes the inclination to pardon the guilty; mercy, the inclination to help the unfortunate. In reality, since the greatest misfortune on earth, the only real misfortune, is to be guilty of sin, one idea calls the other to mind, and the two are so intimately blended that it would be difficult as well as useless to try to distinguish them.

Rather, my child, you should learn from what source they spring.

Why am I inexpressibly clement and merciful?

First of all *because I am inexpressibly holy;* for if sanctity implies a great aversion for sin it implies an equal compassion for the sinner.

According to the Scriptures God is infinite holiness, but also infinite mercy; and the Church adds that His characteristic is "to show mercy and to spare."[1] Jesus is holiness in-

---

[1] Collect, Litany of Saints.

carnate, and you know with what kindness He treated Magdalene, the Samaritan woman, the good thief. After Him, the greatest saints among His disciples showed the most compassion to sinners; witness Francis de Sales, Vincent de Paul, the Curé of Ars.

As Jesus gave me more grace, He also gave me more charity than all the saints together. And this ocean of charity keeps spreading in rivers of clemency and mercy over all who are unhappy.

This incomparable clemency and mercy come to me also *from the fact that I am incomparably a Mother.*

God is no less liberal in the order of grace than in the order of nature. If He has given a wealth of compassion to your mothers so that they are affected by the pains and perils of your mortal bodies, how much more He must have given me so that I am moved to pity over the distress, dangerous in another way, of your souls wounded by sin, enslaved by evil desires, tortured and debased by the devil.

If your mothers, despite their heritage of selfishness from original sin, do not let themselves be disgusted by the most repulsive diseases of their child; if they even become more fondly attached to their child, the more bereft he is; of what shall I not be capable, I whose mother love encounters in my virginal, immaculate heart no division to lessen it, no selfishness to hinder it?

Finally and above all, I am an abyss of clemency and mercy because God, who brings all His wishes into reality, has given me the mission and the power to be the *ambassador* to men *of His pure mercy,* the living image of His infinite clemency.

To be sure, the great envoy of infinite mercy is Jesus, my dear Son. But He remains also the minister of infinite justice: He is appointed your Judge and your Savior at the same time. As for me, I have received the mission and the power of representing and serving nothing but mercy. God never asks me to judge you, to condemn you, to punish you, but only to lift you up again, to heal you, to reconcile you with Him.

This is what wrung a cry of joy and tenderness from the holy Curé of Ars: "Ah! the Blessed Virgin is much better than the best of mothers, for they punish sometimes; she, never!"[2]

Before him another of my great servants, St. Bernard, never grew tired of admiring this function of pure mercy which God has entrusted to me: "Why should human frailty fear to have recourse to Mary? In her is found nothing austere, nothing to terrify: everything about her is full of sweetness. She has for all only the sweetness of milk and the softness of wool. Review carefully in your minds the whole of the gospel narrative, and if you can discover in Mary anything at all that appears reproachful or harsh, or any, even the very least, sign of indignation, look upon her with suspicion for the future and fear to approach her. But ... you find everything that belongs to her full of goodness and grace, redolent of mercy and meekness."[3]

Finally, and with still more authority, the liturgy proclaims that I am meekest of all,[4] sweetness itself,[5] that I have re-

---

[2] Monnin, *Esprit du Curé d'Ars,* p. 87.

[3] *Sermon for the Sunday within the Octave of the Assumption,* #2; in *P. L.,* vol. 183, col. 430; in *St. Bernard's Sermons for the Seasons and Principal Festivals of the Year,* vol. 3, pp. 259-260.

[4] "Inter omnes mitis," in the hymn *Ave Maris Stella.*

[5] "Dulcedo nostra," in the antiphon *Salve Regina.*

ceived a share of sweetness sweeter than honey,[6] that I am
the "Mother of mercy!"[7]

But, you will say, *is she not turned away from poor worms
like us* by the love she has for her Jesus, so lovable and so
loving?

Such would be the case if you were strangers to Jesus. But
since the Redemption has incorporated you into Him, I see
and love in each one of you the true members of Jesus, and
I have no less compassion for your souls debased and tortured
by sin than I felt for the feet and hands of Jesus pierced by
nails or for His beautiful face soiled by spittle.

But, you will say again, does not her incomparable purity
as Virgin and Immaculate inspire in her some repugnance
against bending over souls that have fallen into the mire of
vice?

It is quite true that, far from having the least indulgence
toward sinful habits or attachments, I hold them in horror
and abomination. But this very horror and abomination inspire in me a more poignant compassion for the poor souls
who are slaves of those habits and attachments; for the more
hideous and repulsive I find the leprosy which soils and disfigures them, the more I hasten to purify them of it.

Thus my spotless purity, by making me see more clearly
the great evil that is sin, makes me more compassionate with
regard to those unhappy persons who are the sinners.

It makes me also more powerful to help them. Being immaculate, wholly pure, I was worthy to be associated with
Jesus as victim in that sacrifice of the cross which won all par-

[6] *Ecclus.* 24:27; Epistle of the Motherhood of the Blessed Virgin Mary.
[7] Antiphon *Salve Regina.*

dons for you. Being immaculate and wholly pure, I have enough influence with God to soften His justice when it refuses pardon to you, and enough power to put the devil to flight when he inclines you to repel the advances of God.

In fact, it seems that I have never so multiplied prodigies on behalf of poor sinners as I have since they invoked me under the title of Immaculate: consider the miraculous medal, Lourdes, Fatima.

Since I am the Mother of clemency and of mercy, who never looks at your unworthiness but only at your distress, do not fail to have recourse to me when you must ask for *the graces of which you feel yourself particularly unworthy.*

You do not deserve, for example, that God should release you from the chains of vice or lukewarmness, because it is you yourself that have forged them, link by link, notwithstanding all the reproaches and pleas He kept addressing to your inmost conscience.

You do not deserve that God should give you back the faith or the spirit of faith, because you have committed numerous outrages against that divine light, whether by refusing to follow it or by refusing to look at it or even by seeking to extinguish it through a recurring choice of doubt or denial in practice.

You do not deserve to be delivered from such and such a temptation which harasses you, because it is you yourself that have provoked it by your imprudence, your rashness, your appetite for evil.

You do not deserve that God should grant you such and such a grace, indispensable to fulfill the duties of your state, to answer your vocation, or simply to achieve your salvation, because He has already offered it to you thousands of times and has found in your heart only a beaten path, dry ground, or a soil covered with thorns.

In such a forbidding situation you have only one recourse: to the Mother of mercy, who forgets your guilt and sees only your unhappiness.

Your unhappiness consists in being tied down by the dragging chain of vice or lukewarmness which prevents you from regaining the right road. Beg me to break those formidable bonds: "Solve vincla reis!"[8]

Your unhappiness consists in being like a blind person in the face of supernatural realities. Beg me to obtain light for you: "Profer lumen caecis!"

It is your unhappiness to be cast into the dragon's claws or to be at grips with infinite vengeance. Beg me to rescue you from those adversaries: "Mala nostra pelle!"

It is your unhappiness to have incurred the veto of infinite Justice, who refuses you certain graces because you abuse them. Beg me to have that veto lifted in order that all graces may flow over you anew: "Bona cuncta posce!"

This supplication, my child, bursting forth under the poignantly felt weight of your unworthiness and misery, will never remain unanswered. In her model prayer, "Holy Mary," the Church has you bring forward no other title of recommendation than your unworthiness and misery as a sinner: "Pray for us sinners." While the least self esteem or presumption would tie my hands, the humble confession of your unworthiness permits me to help you in your misery; and however great that misery may be, my mercy will always be greater!

---

[8] Hymn *Ave Maris Stella.*

FAITHFUL VIRGIN

MARY, MODEL OF HUMILITY

NEAR the end of her life St. Therese of the Child Jesus kept repeating, "O God, I beseech You to keep me from being unfaithful!" Asked what type of infidelity she was referring to, she answered, "Of a proud thought voluntarily entertained."[1]

The fact is that a soul established by God in a high degree of perfection cannot deviate from faith except by becoming proud of its very perfection, as did Lucifer, the most perfect of the heavenly spirits.

By contrast, I remained wholly faithful because, under the divine hand which was clothing me with all splendors, graces and privileges, I remained unswervingly humble. It will be to your advantage, my child, to contemplate that ideal humility.

The proud person *is smug in his accomplishments* and his talents, his possessions and his being, as if he had himself to thank for them.

The first use I make of the light with which God enlightens me is to confess that I owe to Him all that I have and all that I am, and to ascribe all the glory of them to Him.

---

[1] *Novissima Verba,* revised translation by the Carmelite nuns of New York (New York: P. J. Kenedy & Sons, 1952), p. 89.

The proud person *finds an intoxicating joy in the honors* bestowed on him.

To me, by contrast, the angel's salutation "Hail, full of grace" brings only disturbance and uneasiness, so permeated am I with my nothingness before God: "My substance is as nothing before You!"[2]

The proud person *appropriates esteem and praise to himself* as something that it due him, forgetting that he owes to God whatever is praiseworthy or estimable about him.

When Elizabeth proclaims me "blessed among women"[3] I cannot deny a praise which I know to be inspired by the Holy Spirit, but I immediately refer it to God without keeping the least bit of it for myself: "My soul magnifies the Lord."[4]

The proud person cannot attain to *a high dignity* without conceiving *a high opinion* of himself.

The dazzling grandeur of my divine motherhood cannot hide my littleness from me, and I can only call myself "the handmaid of the Lord" at the very moment when I am becoming His Mother.

The proud person loses no occasion of *publicizing his honors.*

I speak to no one of the great things God does for me[5] except to Elizabeth and to Joseph, and only after God Himself has told them about these things.

The proud person does not know how *to stoop or to serve.*

Becoming Mother of God does not keep me from being at the service of someone: first of my cousin Elizabeth, then of

[2] *Psalm* 38:6.
[3] *Luke* 1:42.
[4] *Luke* 1:46.
[5] *Luke* 1:49.

my husband Joseph, finally of Jesus and His disciples . . . not
to mention the assistance given on occasion to relatives, to
neighbors, to the poor. Moreover, it is always a question of
rendering the most lowly services to the most lowly people:
lighting the fire, going to draw water, preparing the meals,
washing and mending clothes, maintaining poor cottages in
order and propriety.

The proud person *seeks out places and functions* which
will draw all eyes to him.

During the hidden life of Jesus I do nothing and say
nothing that may distinguish me outwardly from the poor
housewives of Nazareth. During His public life I remain
aside, lost in the crowd of listeners. During the Passion, it
is true, I put myself forward, close to Jesus; but then it is
in order to drink with Him the cup of disgrace, to share with
Him all the shame of the hooting and sarcasm, blows and
spittle! After Pentecost, while the Apostles astonish the world
by their preaching or their miracles, I live so obscure and
hidden, even while being the heart of the young Church, that
the sacred historian never says another word about me.

Those are some of the more evident marks of that humility
which I practiced all my life.

Here are the *principal motives* that inspired my humility
and made impossible for me any impulse of vanity or pride,
however small it might be.

First there is the accurate appraisal of *my condition as
creature.* I see clearly that, compared to the infinite Being
of God, my being is next to nothing. And I see clearly that in
the little that I am, what proceeds from me is only the
nothingness, while everything valuable or praiseworthy I have

proceeds from God. Hence, how could I help ascribing all esteem and praise to God?

Then there is the accurate appraisal of *my condition as daughter of Adam.* I see clearly that without the high privilege of the Immaculate Conception I would have been, like all the other children of Adam, soiled by original sin and infected with the germs of the seven capital sins; I see that without the rampart of actual grace with which God continues to surround me, I would be exposed to falling into imperfection and sin.

Next there is the accurate appraisal of *my condition as first disciple and first member of Christ.*

As a disciple of Christ I feel bound to apply to myself the teachings and examples of that infallible Master and perfect Model. But both the teachings and the examples preach humility before all: "Unless you become like the little children, you shall by no means enter the kingdom of heaven."[6] "The Son of Man has not come to be served, but to serve."[7]

As a member of Christ I feel bound to give way submissively to the impetus of my life principle. And to what would that impetus incline me if not to hunger and thirst after that primordial justice which consists in recognizing God's sovereign rule over us and our radical dependence with regard to Him?

Again, there is the accurate appraisal of *my condition as Co-Redeemer.* Since the first Adam had outraged God and brought about the fall of the human race through pride—"You will be like God"[8]—it is through humility that the

[6] *Matt.* 18:3.
[7] *Matt.* 20:28.
[8] *Gen.* 3:5.

second Adam must repair the outrage committed against God by sin and the damage done by it to man. I feel, therefore, that I can collaborate in this work of reparation and redemption only by embracing, like Jesus, a very humble exterior life and still more humble interior sentiments.

Then there is the accurate appraisal of *my condition as Mother of God*. Since my natural and supernatural lights keep showing me the abyss that exists between Creator and creature, how can I help crying, "Who am I, Lord, that You should see fit to ask me to carry You, to keep You warm, to give You milk, to lavish my cares and caresses on You? Who am I, above all, that You should see fit Yourself, true God of true God, to surround me with a love, a gratitude, an obedience that is truly filial?"

Finally, what makes all pride impossible for me is the accurate appraisal of *the malice of pride*. First, I see clearly how *it outrages God,* how abominable it is to Him, because it proposes to do nothing less than deify the creature. Why indeed does the proud person blind himself to his faults and attribute all His virtues to himself? It is because a God is perfect. Why does he seek to be first in everything? Because a God is above everyone. Why does it go against his grain to show deference or submission to anyone else? Because the first Principle is subordinate to no one. Why does he want to turn everyone's admiration, services and sacrifices to himself? Because all those things are due to the sovereign Good.

I see no less clearly *the harm done to man* by pride. No one can sanctify himself or save himself without grace. Now without humility a person does not think of asking for that indispensable grace: "I am rich ... and have need of nothing."[9] And if he does implore it, he does not deserve to receive it; for he is then the "poor man that is proud,"[10] who loses even the love of compassion, the only kind of love favorable to the wretched. "God resists the proud."[11] He sends them away empty-handed.[12]

Come to me often, my child, to learn these various motives for humility. Falling from my lips, they will appear more persuasive to you. Come to learn by my example the manner of practicing humility. Contemplated in me, this austere virtue becomes sweet and attractive. Above all, come often to imbibe in my heart those choice graces without which humility could neither bud nor increase nor bear fruit in your soul.

[9] *Apoc.* 3:17.
[10] *Ecclus.* 25:4.
[11] *1 Pet.* 5:5.
[12] *Luke* 1:53.

MIRROR OF JUSTICE

MARY, MODEL OF THANKSGIVING

J USTICE is a virtue which inclines a person to give each one his due. You are well enough disposed, my child, to give men what you owe them. You are much less disposed to pay your debts to God, not only those whose payment is difficult or costly, such as adoration and reparation, but even those like gratitude whose payment is easy and pleasant.

In the preface of the Mass the Church declares that "it is truly just and equitable to thank the Lord, always and everywhere." Learn how I practiced, with respect to God, that *supreme justice which is the giving of thanks.*

Enlightened by reason, faith and the gift of knowledge, I saw with perfect clarity that to fail to thank God, our sovereign Benefactor, is to contradict the needs of our rational nature, which makes it a point of honor to respond to every favor with thanks; it is to contradict the exigencies of the grace of Christ, our vital Principle, who urges us to recognize and requite the unceasing goodness of the heavenly Father; it is to contradict the very demands of that infinitely just, infinitely loving Father, which the Apostle Paul formulates in these terms: "In every circumstance give thanks; for this is God's will for you in Christ Jesus."[1]

No less clearly did I see that *this great duty* of thanksgiving *is also a source of great profit.* In the disposition of His favors God looks to His own glory before all. Now to thank Him is to give Him glory and consequently to incline Him to keep giving us more things. And as for ourselves, we cannot give thanks for a grace without making ourselves attentive to it, appreciating its true value and resolving to make it fruitful. And all these dispositions make us worthy to receive graces more abundant and more precious.

With this end in view my soul kept breathing out its gratitude to God as a flower keeps breathing out its scent. The "Magnificat" shows you how I thanked God for the divine motherhood and the other favors that are personal to me. I am going to let you see *how I expressed my thanks to Him* for the favors that are common to you and me together.

"Eternal Father, be thanked for having given me this natural life which exercises itself through the organs of the body and the faculties of the soul . . . but still more for having given me this supernatural life, destined to blossom one day into a life of eternal glory and eternal happiness.

"Be You blessed for having provided for me an inexhaustible reserve of the life-giving air which my lungs breathe . . . but still more for offering me an inexhaustible reserve of graces which my soul breathes through prayer.

"Be You blessed for the fire whose energy, accumulated and imprisoned throughout the years in this piece of wood, now escapes under the form of a beautiful flame which re-

[1] *1 Thess.* 5:18.

joices my eyes and warms my limbs . . . but still more be You thanked for the pure flame of charity which the Holy Spirit is constantly diffusing in my soul in order to enlarge it, to set it on fire, to transform it into Your image.

"Be You blessed for material water, so fresh, so fitted for cooling my body . . . but still more for the water of grace, no less suited to quenching all the thirst of my soul.

"Be You blessed for the light of the heavenly bodies which makes earthly things visible to me . . . but still more for the light of faith which reveals to me supernatural realities incomparably more precious . . . and above all for the light of glory, which will permit me to see face to face Your infinite beauty, Your infinite goodness and the very mystery of Your trinitarian life.

"Be You blessed for these myriads of living seeds which draw upon the energies of the soil and appropriate them to my use by transforming them into plants or fruits . . . but still more for these marvelous seeds of the infused virtues which transform my poor human energies, thoughts, affections and wishes into so many supernatural acts, meriting eternal life.

"Be You blessed for permitting me, for the nourishment of my poor bodily life, to destroy those marvelous living machines which the hand of man could not build: the animals, the birds, the fishes . . . but still more for having willingly permitted that Your own Son be put to death for the preservation of my soul from the death of sin and the liberation of other souls from that death."

I said to Him again: "Eternal Father, how good You are to put to work for us so many men who are Your servants and Your adopted sons . . . and how much better to command Your angels to stand guard at the gate of our souls and to ask Your Son to place at our service, in the Eucharist, all that He has and all that He is.

"How good You are to have given us fellow wayfarers, sharing our faith and our hope, who sustain and console us in our journey across the desert to the promised land . . . and how much better to have willed that Jesus Himself become my Companion in exile by dwelling under my roof, the Companion in exile and in travel of all men by dwelling, through His eucharistic presence, in all parts of the world.

"How good You are to have given us relatives, brothers or sisters, whom the community of blood renders more disposed to cherish and assist us . . . and how much better to have brought it about that every one of Your saints, every one even of Your angels should be true brothers to us, surrounding us with a solicitude and an affection more than brotherly.

"How good You are to have given us a father and a mother to nourish, to guard, to educate our temporal life which is so full of needs, so frail and inexperienced as long as childhood lasts . . . and how much better to have seen fit Yourself to become our true Father by making us participate in Your divine life and harboring truly paternal sentiments toward us.

"How good You are to give married people children to continue their name and their race and to owe them affection, gratitude, assistance . . . and how much better to give the power to all Your faithful, especially to all who are consecrated to You, to beget into everlasting life (through their prayer, their apostolate, their sacrifice) numerous souls who will recognize in heaven that they are obliged to them for their salvation and will show them everlasting affection and gratitude.

"Thank You finally, eternal Father, for having given us a temporal fatherland and a temporal city in which we find teachers to instruct us, rulers to govern us, soldiers to defend us, an immeasurable heritage of goods of every sort accumulated by hundreds of generations . . . and thank You still more for having made us members of a spiritual fatherland and city, where Your only Son becomes in person our Teacher, our Guide, our Defender, and where we find an inexhaustible heritage of supernatural goods, amassed by Christ and His saints, the least of which is worth more than all the goods of nature combined."[2]

Those, my child, are some verses of the *psalm of thanksgiving* which I kept singing to God in my heart.

Now it is the role of mothers to serve as a model to their little ones. Make it your aim, therefore, following my example, to keep thanking your heavenly Father for the two-fold banquet of grace and of nature to which He invites you at every moment.

It is the province of mothers to teach their children to say thank you. Ask me every day, then, to obtain for you a large share of my spirit of thanksgiving, that is to say, the spirit of faith which knows how to perceive divine Providence behind the curtain of creatures, ever intent on doing good to you; the spirit of charity, which lets itself be affected by the least favor; the spirit of generosity, which inclines one to repay favors.

[2] St. Thomas, *Summa Theologica,* Ia IIae, q. 93, a. 9 ad 2um.

Finally, it is the function of mothers to make up for their children's negligence or weakness. To compensate for the unworthiness or the unimportance of your thanksgiving, especially after a more exceptional benefit such as Communion, do not grow tired of offering God that thanks which I keep repeating to Him for you and which He finds so pleasing.

SEAT OF WISDOM

MARY, MODEL OF OBEDIENCE

T RUE wisdom, for a rational creature, is *to conform one-self to the Creator's will,* whether by carrying out carefully the orders and desires He makes known to us through laws and superiors, or by accepting with patience the way of life and of death which His good pleasure has decreed for each one of us.

Waiting for another occasion (Queen of Confessors) to tell you the nature of my abandonment to God's good pleasure, I am going to teach you, my child, the nature of *my obedience* to His orders and His desires.

First of all, my obedience was wholly *supernatural,* grounded in the spirit of faith.

That faith, always alert, allowed me to discern the authentic expression of the divine will in every precept of the Law, in every command of superiors.

Under that veil, sometimes quite opaque, I adored the will of the sovereign Master who has an absolute right to obedience from His creatures, made by Him and for Him. I adored the will of the sovereign Judge who abstains, here below, from exacting that obedience by force, to reserve for us the honor and the merit of giving it freely to Him, but determined to punish severely the rash and impious one who would refuse it.

Above all, under each of those precepts or injunctions I adored the completely lovable will of our Father in heaven, who sees fit thus to dam up the whole course of our free activity, in order to prevent its being lost or swallowed up, and to direct it by the shortest, surest way to the eternal fatherland.

Inspired by such motives, my obedience could not be other than *total*: I obeyed with my whole soul.

As soon as an order or a prohibition begins to restrict your freedom, you readily indulge in secret complaints or open criticisms which will discredit the order in your eyes and those of your brethren. In any case it is hard for you to give the order the full consent of your mind before examining its rights and understanding the motives which justify it.

My mind, in contrast, had too clear a view of God's absolute sovereignty to dare utter the least murmur against His precept, even when I was clearly exempt from it, as I was from the precept of the Purification; even when it demanded of me more than life, as did the precept of the Passion and death imposed on my dear Son.

And likewise I had too clear a view of God's unfailing wisdom not to admit immediately and without proof the justice and the timeliness of His prescriptions.

To the total consent of my mind I joined the total consent of the heart. At all times I entertained in my heart a burning love for the divine commands, formulated in the Law and the prophets. Like the psalmist, whose sentiments and words I made my own, I loved the divine precepts more than gold and precious stones,[1] I cherished them passionately,[2] I carried them in my heart[3] as the dominant affection which subordinates all the rest. Hence I was eager to know them always better, and I asked for this grace: "Lord, give me discernment that I may know Your decrees."[4] They were the object of my meditation all day long,[5] the joy of my heart,[6] whereas I was consumed with anger and shed streams of tears[7] to see them forgotten and violated by so many of my brethren.

Loving God's orders and desires thus with all my heart, I could only fulfill them with all my heart, *through love and with love.*

Mine, therefore, was a disinterested obedience, not that of a mercenary, motivated by fear of punishment or the enticement of a wage, but that of a loving child, solely concerned with pleasing her heavenly Father.

It was also a prompt obedience; for love does not have to be called twice: at the first sign from the Beloved it rises, it runs, it flies, breaking all shackles, sweeping away all obstacles.

It was a diligent, careful obedience; for love dreads the least negligence, the least defect that might displease the Beloved.

Finally, it was a joyful obedience: love feels no pain;

---

[1] *Psalm* 118:127.
[2] *Psalm* 118:40.
[3] *Psalm* 39:9.
[4] *Psalm* 118:125.
[5] *Psalm* 118:97.
[6] *Psalm* 118:111.
[7] *Psalm* 118:136,139.

or, if it feels pain, it is happy to spend itself and exhaust itself for the Beloved.

Since it proceeded from my reverence toward the sovereign Master and my love for the heavenly Father, my obedience could not be other than *universal,* extending without exception to all the divine wishes, all equally lovable and adorable.

Thus, whereas you are inclined to despise *the little precepts* of the law or of superiors, under the pretext that they are without importance, I took special pleasure in fulfilling all of them with care.

The fact is that these little observances, imposed on me every day and every hour, supplied me with the occasion of offering God constantly renewed evidences of my gratitude and my filial love. These evidences were nevertheless very deserving of merit; for only a watchful, delicate love is able to discern under the commonplace mask of little things that greatest thing of all which is the will of the Master, the will of the Father.

Hence how could I help being indignant (and how can I help being indignant still today) at hearing that pitiful excuse: "It's such a little thing!"

Indeed? Is it a small matter to shrug your shoulders at an order or a desire of Jesus? Is it a small matter to lose an occasion of giving Him pleasure and cause Him displeasure instead? Is it a small matter to let go of the grace and the merit He has attached to this little observance? Is it a small matter to have reinforced the tendency of desire to be aroused and the tendency of the will to surrender? To be sure, each little disobedience, taken by itself, may have only an infinitesimal effect; but does not experience prove that infinitely small things when multiplied may amount to a great deal of evil?

Through inattention or lack of reflection you neglect the little observances; through laziness you seek to escape *those that are burdensome.*

The Mosaic Law imposed heavy sacrifices on me; and God Himself imposed others incomparably heavier, for example, the Passion and death of my Son. But the more my nature protested, the more my love urged me to consent fully to all the divine demands: Father, not my will but Yours."[8]

The fact is that the more costly was obedience, the more certainty I had that I was seeking God's good pleasure alone, and the more this obedience permitted me to offer the Beloved an excellent gift: not only my work and my application, but my suffering, my life strength and all those other goods, including Jesus, of which I had not the right to dispose by myself.

Finally, you find it hard to fulfill the divine commands when they are *made known to you through human intermediaries.*

Although I often had to deal with civil or religious authorities who deserved neither sympathy nor esteem, I obeyed them willingly, with the thought that I was thereby bearing witness to a more perfect love for God. For, just as it is the property of delicate love to obey in the smallest things and of strong love to obey in the hardest things, so it is the property of love unfailing to obey the divine will even when

8 *Luke* 22:42.

it is hidden under the shabby dress of a human will, fallible, clumsy or brutal.

My child, do you want to make yourself capable of obeying in everything and with your whole soul? Strive to *discern, as I did,* the presence of the divine will in every prescription of the law or every command of a superior; the greatness of the divine will in what appears to you small and petty in those orders; the wisdom of the divine will in what seems to you hardly justified in them; the lovableness and sweetness of the divine will in their hardest requirements.

CAUSE OF OUR JOY

MARY, DISPENSER OF TRUE JOYS

T HE *first ray of joy,* awaited for thousands of years, which infinite Mercy caused to shine before the eyes of fallen humanity, *was the Incarnation of the Word.* "And the Word became flesh, and dwelt among us."[1] "And the angel said to them, 'Behold, I bring you good tidings of a great joy.' "[2]

It is to me, my child, after God, that you are indebted for this joy. For the eternal Word, considering it unworthy of Himself and of me to become flesh in my womb without my knowledge or against my will, chose to make my consent, fully conscious and free, the indispensable condition of His Incarnation.

It is thanks to my "Be it done," therefore, that you can rejoice in having an ideal Teacher to make known to you the Father "whom no one knows except the Son";[3] an ideal Model to show you how a true son must revere, love and serve that Father; an ideal Leader to draw you after Him

[1] *John* 1:14.
[2] *Luke* 2:10.
[3] *Matt.* 11:27.

in the rough way of virtue and perfection; an ideal Pontiff
to offer to the Father in your name a homage of adoration
and thanksgiving, love and prayer, worthy of His infinite
majesty; finally and above all, an ideal Mediator, alone
capable (by satisfying for the infinite outrage of sin) of
reconciling you with that most lovable Father and meriting
for you a heritage of grace and glory.

In short, the Word could not be all those things to you
except by means of that human body, subject to suffering and
death, which He asked of me and which I gave Him know-
ingly and freely: "Behold the handmaid of the Lord; be it
done to me according to your word."[4]

The second ray of joy which infinite Mercy caused to shine
in this world of darkness *was the superabundant Redemption,*
brought about through the merits of Christ.

And, because I was associated throughout the redemptive
work, meriting for you with a merit of equity all the pardons
and graces that Christ was meriting for you in justice, I contributed in a very real manner to acquiring for you all the
joys of which the Redemption is the source.

Those joys are beyond number and beyond telling: the
joy of having been able to climb out of the pit in which sin
was holding you chained and which death would have closed
irrevocably over your heads; the joy of having been freed
from the cruel tyranny of the devil and the debasing slavery
of evil inclinations; the joy of being incorporated into Christ
Jesus as His true members and consequently of being made
partakers of the divine life He Himself receives from His
Father; the joy of becoming, like Christ, the true temples of

---

[4] *Luke* 1:38.

the three divine Persons and of enjoying their intimacy and their assistance without interruption; the joy of forming but one body in Christ with all the holy souls of earth, purgatory and heaven and of profiting, in consequence, by their patronage, their merit and their more than brotherly affection; the joy of being co-heirs with Christ and of being called one day to share His power and His triumph, His glory and His everlasting happiness.

Following the example of the saints, do not fail to thank me for these various joys, so precious and acquired at so great a price, the price of my agony on Calvary.

The third ray of joy which infinite Mercy caused to shine on your poor earth *was the descent of the Holy Spirit,* coming to inaugurate the superabundant dispensation of graces proper to the new alliance: "With joys profuse the world exults."[5]

Now just as my prayer in the cenacle drew the Holy Spirit and His gifts irresistibly down upon the newly founded Church,[6] so my prayer in heaven calls the Holy Spirit and His graces upon each particular soul "when I will, as I will, as much as I will."[7]

And you may imagine what a new flowering of joys such a bestowal can bring about in your soul!

You bewail your childish ignorance and helplessness, which prevent you from properly nourishing your spiritual life. What a joy it is to know that I am constantly bent over your soul like a tender nurse, to obtain for it at the right time the indispensable food of grace, accommodating that food to all the littlenesses of your mind, your heart and your will!

[5] Preface of Pentecost.
[6] Pius XII, *On the Mystical Body,* #110.
[7] St. Bernardine of Siena, *Sermo* 5; in *Opera Omnia,* vol. 4, p. 93.

You fear your childish inexperience and heedlessness, which prevent you from seeing or avoiding the many traps constantly set for you by the flesh, the world and the devil. What a joy it is to know that I am always at your side like a watchful guardian, to remove the stumbling-block from your path, to make Satan let go of you when he presses too close, or to offer you, in my arms and on my heart, the surest of refuges against the assault of your enemies!

You bewail your childish clumsiness, weakness and cowardice, which prevent you from making rapid progress in the rough way of the virtues. What a joy it is to see me always walking before you to draw you on, by my example and my grace, in the way of piety and charity, purity and humility!

You bewail your inability to guide and help the souls under your charge. What a joy it is to see me place my all-powerful intercession at your disposal, to preserve the innocence of those children exposed to so many dangers, to rescue those sinners from the abyss of their sinful habits, to strengthen those dying persons in the lists where they are fighting alone the decisive battle, and even to go and comfort that departed soul in the prison of purgatory which you cannot enter!

With still more reason you are distressed to see yourself incorrigibly prone to squander the same graces every day, to commit the same faults every day. What a joy it is to know that I am authorized by God Himself to draw upon His infinite mercy and keep obtaining new pardons and new graces for you!

The Holy Spirit, by the mouth of the Apostle, advises Christians to keep cultivating spiritual joy, the better to defend themselves against carnal and sinful joys, the more easily to muster all their energies to the service of God, to make their brethren happier and their religion more attractive.

You should know that infinite Mercy has given me to Christians as *a source of joy, accessible at all times and to all the powers of their soul.*

I am a source of joy for your senses, your memory, your imagination; for I offer myself to them as the most beautiful creature, but of a beauty which, far from disturbing them, is wonderfully designed, to pacify, purify, rectify and ennoble them.

I am a source of joy for your mind, which readily lets itself be captivated by the splendor of my privileges: "A great sign appeared in heaven: a woman clothed with the sun, and the moon was under her feet, and upon her head a crown of twelve stars."[8]

Above all, I am a source of joy for your heart. Your heart finds joy in being loved. I am the most loving of mothers, surrounding you always with an incomparable tenderness: an unfailing love rebuffed by no ugliness, discouraged by no ingratitude; an ardent, tender love next to which any affection coming from another creature will be only burned-out ashes. Your heart finds joy in loving. Where could you find a mother more lovable, more approachable to put up with your defects, more clement to pardon your faults, more devoted to provide for all your needs, more compassionate to dry your tears and console you in your childish griefs?

Then resolve at all times, my child, but especially when sadness begins to overgrow the various faculties of your soul, to come and water them in this every flowing source of pure joy.

[8] *Apoc.* 12:1.

SPIRITUAL VESSEL

MARY, FULL OF GRACE

THE holy Doctors, my child, love to call me "spiritual vessel" because in a transcendent way I possessed the Holy Spirit and the supernatural goods which He pours into the soul of the just person.

The Trinity dwells in "light inaccessible."[1] But when It raises us to the supernatural state, It *comes to abide in our soul as in Its temple,* to surrender Itself to our poor embrace: "We will come to him and make Our abode with him."[2]

Now whereas other souls must await the justification of Baptism to enter into possession of that valued Presence, thanks to the privilege of my Immaculate Conception I have enjoyed it from the very first moment of my existence. Surrounded from that first instant by the light of the divine Guest, my soul never knew that horrible night which is the absence of the Holy Spirit; not for a single hour, not a single minute, was it a "daughter of darkness."

While others of the just are always in danger, as long as

[1] *1 Tim.* 6:16.
[2] *John* 14:23.

126

they travel the paths of exile, of committing some grave sin which will drive the Holy Spirit from the temple of their soul and bring in the devil, I was wholly exempted from that frightful misfortune by the jealous love of the three divine Persons, which surrounded me, as it were, with a triple wall of flame, absolutely impregnable to the devil and his agents.

Finally, while others of the just (save for the rare privileged ones who reach the summit of mystical union) are unconscious of the divine Guest's presence in the sanctuary of their soul, the three Persons of the Trinity favored me by making Their presence and Their embrace more or less tangible to me throughout my life.

But the Holy Spirit, not content with making my soul His temple of predilection, pours into it *a fulness of grace* greater than that of the angels and saints combined, because for Him to love is to give, and He loves me more than all the angels and saints together.

Habitual grace is a partaking of the divine nature.[3] As the action of a flame makes metal like fire, the presence of the Trinity in my soul confers on it a divine resemblance by making it glow with divine beauty and splendor.

In the lukewarm person this irradiation may be compared to a brilliant, burning point in the midst of a cold, dark mass.

In the fervent person it extends progressively to all the faculties of the soul, but encounters points of resistance to the divine light, which constitute so many blemishes and deformities: the seven capital sins.

[3] *2 Pet.* 1:4.

In the perfect soul these seven evil roots are destroyed by the Holy Spirit's devouring flame, but the world and the devil still succeed in tarnishing the soul's splendor with the dust of imperfections.

By contrast, in my immaculate soul the irradiation of the divine Guest encounters no opaque point, for I am exempt from every evil inclination, innate or acquired. And its glow is not obscured by any dust, for I am exempt from all venial sin and every imperfection.

Granted the same holds true for the angels and saints in heaven, nevertheless God perceives more beauty and takes more delight in my soul alone than in all of them. The reason is that each class of angels or saints has the mission of reflecting especially one divine perfection: virgins reflect purity; martyrs, strength; cherubim, wisdom; seraphim, love. To me it has been given to reflect them all, to be the masterpiece in which are condensed all the divine rays dispersed over other creatures.

To this fulness of grace is joined *a fulness of virtues* no less admirable.

Just as the graft, by drawing on the bitter sap of the wild stock, transforms it into delicious fruits, so the infused virtues, engrafted on our intellect and our will, have the power of supernaturalizing all our free acts and making them meritorious for heaven.

In the lukewarm person the supernatural graft of the virtues, remaining no more than a sprout, draws out only an insignificant part of the soul's energies; the rest is usurped by the wild shoots of the natural inclinations or the poisonous vegetations of evil desires.

In the fervent and the perfect soul, the bulk of the thoughts and affections is indeed drained by this graft; but the wild stock, the old man, does not stop levying a more or less sizable tribute.

In my immaculate soul there never arose a thought or an aspiration, an affection or a choice which was not immediately seized by the graft of the virtues. Never did the least pursuance of my own will enter in to vitiate my intention by mingling with the pursuit of the divine will. And in the execution of that will, never did the attraction of any pleasure or the fear of any suffering enter in to become the occasion of the least delay or neglect.

Not only were my virtues never halted or slowed down in their flight towards the sovereign Good by the obstruction of any evil desire, but they kept tending towards that Good with a speed and a strength unknown even to the angels.

The reason is that the eternal Word, who loves me more than all the angels and saints, conferred on me from the first moment a charity which makes me capable of loving Him more than all the angels and saints combined.

And the other virtues, receiving their life and movement from charity, could not but partake of its strength and sovereign sway. When God asked me to deliver Jesus in order to serve His redemptive plan, my fortitude enabled me to face all the anguish, all the shame, all the sorrow; my temperance enabled me to go against the most irresistible urges of mother love; my justice enabled me to pay a reparation as costly as the Passion and death of my dear Son to restore to God the glory taken away by your sins.

Thus, to make me worthy of being His Mother, the Word

conferred on me from the first moment of my existence a fulness of grace and virtue, the extent of which not even the angels could measure. Nevertheless, He desired that *this fulness keep increasing* right up to my last breath.

Grace increases through prayer and merit. You will not find it hard to understand that my prayer and my merit were constant. Would you like to get some idea of their value? Start with this principle: the reward of grace that God assigns to a prayer or a good work is measured by the degree of pleasure He finds in the supplication and in the suppliant, in the meritorious act and in its author.

Now Christ was inexpressibly pleased by my person, because He saw in me the purest, fairest reflection of His eternal beauty and, above all, because I was His Mother, His true Mother wholly lovable and wholly loving.

He was inexpressibly pleased with my prayer, for no other could be humbler, more confident, more ardent, more persevering, more respectful; and equally pleased with my good works, all in the direct service of His Person or His redemptive work, and as perfect as possible both in intention and in execution.

Moreover, from the time of the Incarnation the Word was pleased to confer on me unending increases of grace which I had neither deserved nor implored; it was His royal, divine way of paying me for each new service.

In certain more decisive circumstances these waves of grace became a deluge. If one Communion or one Mass can enrich you with graces and virtues, what a flood of grace and virtue I must have received in that incomparable communion of nine months during which I carried the Word incarnate in my womb, in that supreme Mass of Calvary where I was so intimately associated with Jesus!

On the day of my conception the angels had admired the fulness of my initial grace: "Who is she that comes forth as the dawn?"[4] On the day of my Assumption the fulness of my final grace enraptures them: "Who is she that comes up out of the desert . . . perfumed with myrrh and frankincense and all the powders . . . ?"[5]

As for you, my child, when you salute me fifty times a day as "full of grace," do not fail to rejoice and to congratulate me, with the angels, on the fact that the Holy Spirit has clothed me with such supernatural beauty and perfection.

And when you say "Mother of God, pray for us," ask me to obtain for you a large measure of grace and virtue, the only possessions worthy of adorning the temple of your soul and of meriting divine approval, the only goods that can escape the ravages of death and change into life everlasting.

[4] *Cant.* 6:9; Communion of the Vigil of the Immaculate Conception.
[5] *Cant.* 3:6; feast of the Assumption, 1st nocturn, 1st responsory.

VESSEL OF HONOR

MOTIVES FOR DEVOTION TO MARY

T WO strong motives urge you, my child, to honor me with greater devotion every day: *the will of Jesus, the interests of your soul.*

Jesus wants you to show affection, gratitude and respect for those whom He has given you as parents, benefactors, leaders. Am I not *your Mother, your Benefactor, your Sovereign*: a Sovereign ever bent on defending you from a world of enemies, a Benefactor always concerned with obtaining indispensable grace for you, a Mother who constantly carries your soul in the womb of her tenderness and solicitude until she has given it birth into life everlasting?

Jesus wants you to *imitate the saints,* the living copies of Himself. Speaking of the saints that preceded him, St. Bonaventure affirms that he knows of none who did not have a great devotion to me.[1] This is still more true of the ones who followed him, for example those prelates and founders of

[1] *Sermo* 2 *in Purificatione Beatae Mariae Virginis!* in *Opera Omnia* (Florence: Quaracchi), vol. 9, p. 559.

Orders, burdened with occupations, like St. Pius V, St. Robert Bellarmine, St. Charles Borromeo, St. Francis de Sales, St. Ignatius Loyola, St. Vincent de Paul, St. John Eudes, St. Alphonsus de Liguori, who made it a rule to offer me the tribute of a rosary every day.

Jesus wants you to *follow the directives of His Church.* And the Church exerts herself in every way to inculcate a great devotion to me. She does it through the teaching of her Popes: ten encyclicals of Leo XIII on the rosary; through numerous feasts to honor my mysteries in parallel with those of Jesus: seventeen for the universal Church, twenty others for particular regions; through the sanctuaries she dedicates to me: thirty-four cathedral churches in France alone;[2] through the many practices she approves and encourages: eighty indulgenced prayers, eight scapulars, May devotions, special devotions for the month of the rosary and the first Saturday of each month; finally, through the thirty archconfraternities and the hundred and fifty Congregations instituted under my name with the aim of forming a choice group of souls eminently "Mary's."

Above all, Jesus wants you to *imitate His own example*: "As I have done ... so you also should do."[3] "Be minded as was Christ Jesus."[4]

If you consider His deeds and His attitudes, you will see that He consecrated thirty of the thirty-three years of His life to me: as a child He gives you the example of a total dependence on me; as an adult, the example of a total devotion to my service.

[2] Forty-two in the United States and its territories.
[3] *John* 13:15.
[4] *Phil.* 2:5.

If you examine His heart you will see resplendent in their ideal perfection all the forms of filial devotion: tenderness, gratitude, respect. And in heaven that divine Heart remains always animated by the same sentiments and always eager, especially at the moment of Communion, to pour them into your heart.

But *why is Jesus so desirous* of seeing me honored by all of you?

First, *out of love for me.* To my loving, sensitive Son it is intolerable that His fellow men have only forgetfulness and ingratitude towards me. As my loving Spouse[5] He wants me to share all His possessions and especially the tribute of praise, reverence and affection which all creatures owe Him.

But it is also *out of love for Himself;* for He knows in advance that I shall send up to Him every act of affection or praise addressed to me by men and angels and that, far from keeping the least part of them, I shall join to them the priceless increase of my own admiration and my own love.

In proclaiming me "blessed among women" St. Elizabeth made the "Magnificat" spring from my heart. Similarly, the effect of the poor prayers and praises that you address to me is to release my prayer and my praise, so agreeable in God's sight that He has been pleased to answer them throughout the centuries with a flowering of miracles.

To cultivate devotion to me, then, is to give great pleasure to Jesus. It is also to do *great good to your soul,* for there is *no surer way,* no swifter, easier way to acquire the good things of Jesus: His grace, His virtues, His intimate friendship, His paradise.

[5] Son, on the level of nature; Spouse, on the level of grace.

A little child left to himself cannot travel far without getting his clothes dirty and torn; and if the path is next to a cliff and is strewn with traps, it will not be long before he suffers a fatal accident. On the other hand, if he is guided and upheld by his mother, he easily escapes all these dangers, whether he notices them or not.

One who has merited my help through a sincere, persevering devotion travels no less securely on the path of virtue or perfection. While others of keener vision let themselves be led astray by the worst illusions, this little one, enlightened by my light, immediately sees through the mirages of the flesh, the world or the devil. And while others better disciplined surrender before a pleasure too fascinating for them or a threat too formidable, this little one, upheld by my grace of fortitude, resists victoriously all the tempter's enticements and all his violence.

It may happen indeed that he exposes his spiritual life to final disaster through his own fault, whether by having neglected to feed it on the Sacraments or exercise it by the practice of the virtues, or by having weakened it with the wounds of numerous venial sins, or by having thrust it into the occasion of sin himself. In all these cases he would have no right to the help of the grace he has so culpably neglected or opposed. Nonetheless, I will be sure to obtain it for him, because as a loving Mother I do not let myself be outdone in generosity; because as Mother of mercy I never abandon those who trust in me, whatever be their wretched state.

Besides being the surest way I am also *the shortest way* of going to Jesus.

If a person wants to sail swiftly towards Christian or religious perfection, despite the contrary currents of fallen nature, he must join to the exercise of the virtues, which finds its analogy in the slow action of the oars, the exercise of the gifts of the Holy Spirit, comparable to the breath of the wind in the sails. See how the Apostles, so imperfect until then, reached the summit of Christian and priestly perfection in one bound as soon as the Pentecostal Spirit carried them away with His irresistible breathing.

But was it not my prayer, with more power than any other, that drew the divine Spirit upon the cenacle? And if He continued to pour out so many miracles and graces on the young Church, was it not because my presence made it more beautiful and more lovable in His eyes than the assembly of the angels!

Proportionately, it is the same with every soul that makes me live and reign in itself through a sincere devotion: it exercises an irresistible attraction on the Holy Spirit. Wherever that divine Spirit sees me invoked, loved and served, He hastens with the abundance of His gifts,[6] which crush all resistance and quickly impel the soul into the footsteps of Jesus.

Finally, though it is a very sure and a very short way, devotion to me remains *a very sweet way*.

No one carries on the battle of the faith without effort or suffering. I sweeten the bitterness of the effort required by the practice of piety or virtue, by adding to it some drops of sensible consolation, for "my spirit is sweeter than honey."[7] I offer myself to your soul as an ever approachable hearth

---

[6] St. Grignion de Montfort, *Treatise on the True Devotion to the Blessed Virgin Mary*, #36, p. 28.

[7] *Ecclus.* 24:27; Epistle of the Motherhood of the Blessed Virgin Mary.

of consolation and joy, for I reflect the sweetness of God in a way so vivid and so adjusted to your mortal eyes that you cannot help feeling it as soon as you place yourself within the radiant glow of my virtues or my mysteries.

In the same way I sweeten the bitterness of suffering by persuading the divine Sculptor to work with a gentler hand, or at least to intensify His grace in the measure in which He intensifies His blows.

Convinced of the advantages obtained by devotion to me, labor without respite, my child, to root that devotion ever deeper in each of your faculties: senses, heart, intellect, will. It will be like planting balm and myrrh to purify their polluted atmosphere, like planting olive trees to make their unused energies bear fruit in merits, like planting roses to clothe them all with a magnificent flowering of virtues which will draw down on them the heavenly Father's approval and favors.

FAMED VESSEL OF DEVOTION

MARY'S PRAYER FOR US

To the saints and angels my heart appears as a spring from which there wells an uninterrupted flood of praise, thanksgiving and prayer. Among these different sentiments of devotion it is particularly easy and useful for you, my child, to contemplate my prayer, and especially *my prayer as universal Mediatrix.*

In the first place it is a supplication of unbelievable *breadth.* At every moment it sends up before God more desires and requests than the drops of water cast skyward by a fountain.

Among the mass of men dispersed over the face of the earth, some, faithful and religious, convey their distress in more or less fervent supplications addressed to God, to me or to the saints. I gather up every one of these supplications, be it only a cry or a sigh, and, after purifying all in the fire of my charity, send them up before God as an incense of agreeable odor.

That is why the liturgy compares me to the sweet smelling plants that transform the common juices of the soil into delicate aromas: "I took root in an honorable people.[1] I gave forth a sweet fragrance like cinnamon and aromatic balm. I yielded a sweet smell like choicest myrrh."[2]

But most men, unfortunately, do not know how to convey in prayer the needs or the perils of their souls. Often they are no longer even aware of those needs or perils, like the seriously ill who no longer feel the fever that is consuming them or the abscess devouring them or the chill of death creeping over them.

In the light of God I perceive distinctly each one of those hidden or unknown troubles, and the ardent compassion I feel for each of them is expressed immediately by an appeal to infinite Mercy. Just as the nerves feel and transmit to the brain the needs of those millions of little cells that compose the human organism, so I feel through my mother love and transmit to God through my prayer all the troubles of those millions of beings composing the human race, which has become the mystical body of Christ.

Although it extends to all men, my prayer remains as *intense and fervent* as if it concerned only one.

Imagine a loving mother with her child tortured by hunger or suspended over a cliff or carried away by a wild animal. With what ardor and vehemence she would implore help or delivery for him!

To every man, whoever he may be, I am the ideal Mother: the most clearsighted to discern his least obvious needs or dangers, the most sympathetic to feel them as if they were my own, the most devoted to obtain effective aid for him at any price.

[1] *Ecclus.* 24:16; Little Office of the Blessed Virgin Mary, 2nd lesson.
[2] *Ecclus.* 24:20; Little Office of the Blessed Virgin Mary, 3rd lesson.

And so I am bound to put all the ardor of my soul into the prayer I address to God for each one of my children:

"Eternal Father, I see the just, the object of all my love, desirous but incapable of struggling up the rugged path of the virtues. Please give them in abundance their daily bread: those graces of light and strength which will permit them to attain the degree of perfection and beatitude You have assigned them.

"Eternal Father, I see the lukewarm, the object of my solicitude, on the point of being swallowed up in the mire of their lust, or of being contaminated by a corrupt world, or of falling into a subtle trap the devil has laid for them. Please shelter these heedless, imprudent, rash children under the wings of Your protection.

"Eternal Father, I see the sinners, object of my compassion, become slaves of the impure spirit. I see with what fury he soils them, debases them, tortures and drags them ever lower into the depths of the abyss, awaiting only the hour of death to cast them down finally. Please, despite their wickedness, have pity on these unhappy ones and 'save them from the lion's mouth!' "[3]

The same mother love that makes my prayer ardent also makes it *persevering*.

Because I am Mother, and Mother of mercy, nothing can discourage the prayer which I pray unceasingly for my children.

The good are continually wasting, through frailty, a large part of the choice graces I obtain for them. I keep praying that those graces may be offered them once more.

The mediocre through laziness neglect to answer the gentle

[3] *Psalm* 21:22.

call which the Holy Spirit causes to sound always at the door of their heart. I never tire of imploring for them a more powerful grace, capable of jolting them out of their lethargy.

The wicked, because of their perverse passions, insist on rejecting the graces of repentance I obtain for them, and even on opposing them, throwing themselves from one defilement into another. With even greater insistence I lodge an appeal for them with infinite Mercy, that It may draw them out of that hardness of heart which is a prelude to damnation.

However ardent and insistent it may be, my prayer for you remains *very humble.*

It is humble because I have a very clear vision of the infinite Grandeur which I implore. "Lord," I say with the prophet, "I am as nothing before You. All my perfection, joined to that of the angels, stands in comparison to Yours like a drop of water forgotten on the edge of a vessel, a grain of dust lying unobserved on the tray of a scale.[4] I pray You, however, to listen to me by reason of Your goodness and Your mercy, which are also without limit.

"My prayer becomes still humbler, Lord, when I consider that no creature could have any right to the goods I implore: divine friendship and sonship, grace and glory. These indeed are supernatural goods which all the sacrifices of men, all the services of the angels and all the love of the seraphim could not adequately merit!

"It is not enough to say that my children have no title to them: they are positively unworthy of them. What are my children, indeed, for the most part, if not rebellious servants,

[4] *Is.* 40:15.

even now engaged in soiling, debasing and turning against You the talents with which You have enriched them? Or if not rebellious, at least they are ungrateful servants who do not know how to appreciate Your gifts: Gospel, Mass, Sacraments; lazy, idle servants, more careful of their ease than of Your service; unbecoming servants, more concerned with their interests than with Your glory."

As humble as my prayer becomes in consideration of your wretchedness, it is equally *confident* in consideration of infinite Mercy.

My first motive for confidence is that God Himself has appointed me your Advocate. I need not inquire whether it is through your own fault that you are wretched. It is enough for me to know that you are. Then I have the mandate and the power of recommending you to infinite Mercy, the more insistently as your misery is greater.

My second motive for confidence is that Jesus places His satisfactions and His merits at my disposal. Why should I not ask pardon and grace for all of you with assurance when I can offer God in exchange the infinite satisfactions of Jesus, which give Him more glory than all sins combined can take away from Him, or the infinite merits of Jesus, which are worth incomparably more than all graces together, however precious they may be?

There, my child, is a pale glimpse of my prayer as universal Suppliant.

Be pleased to recall it often, that you may arouse yourself to bless God for having given poor human beings so perfect an Advocate; that you may learn from my example to extend your compassion to all the members of the mystical body and

to recommend their distress to God with fervor and perseverance, confidence and humility; above all that you may
offer my prayer to infinite Justice and infinite Mercy, in order
to make up for the insufficiency or the unworthiness of your
own intercession on behalf of souls.

MYSTICAL ROSE

MARY AND THE LOVE OF GOD

S INCE the time of my sojourn on earth I have been pre-eminently the mystical Rose, first because of *the extent of my love.*

Just as a rose bush drains the most varied juices from the soil in which it is rooted and transforms them all into roses, so holy charity jealously drained all thoughts from my mind, all decisions from my will, all recollections from my memory— in a word, all the energies of my being, to transform them all into acts of pure love.

The other saints find it very hard to love God with all their heart: they always discover some part that continues to beat with self love.

In my virginal, immaculate heart the love of God always reigned supreme. No other love ever tried to invade that garden enclosed, that paradise of delights which the cherubim's sword, turning every way, guards for God alone.[1]

If the other saints do come to love God with their whole

[1] *Gen.* 3:24.

heart, they never succeed in loving Him with their whole mind, their whole soul, their whole strength. For, like thorns which dispute the energies of the soil with the good seed, the seven captial sins (even mortified and reduced to germinal state) keep usurping for the benefit of self love a good part of the thoughts of their mind, the dreams of their imagination, the emotions of their senses.

In me, on the other hand, that same love which reigned supreme over my heart had no difficulty in subjecting the other powers to itself, because it found there no opposition of the seven evil desires, from which my Immaculate Conception had totally preserved me.

Under the sweet but irresistible impulse of divine love my mind was perpetually absorbed in the thought of God, present in my soul by the state of grace, present in the dear Son I clasped in my arms, present in creatures, each one of which revealed to me a ray of His wisdom or His kindness.

Under that same impulse my memory, my imagination and my senses were always in search of God, the sole object of my joys and sorrows, my fears and hopes; and if they rested for a moment on creatures, it was only to seek there a reflection of the face of God, who clothes them with beauty merely by fixing His gaze on them.[2]

Thus when the Judge, at the end of my life, scrutinized the stuff of my interior conversation, in which were woven so many thoughts and memories, dreams and emotions, desires and resolutions, He found in it not a single thread that was not of pure gold: truly I gave God nothing but love.

[2] St. John of the Cross, *Spiritual Canticle,* stanza 5; in *The Complete Works of St. John of the Cross,* vol. 2, p. 50.

And when He examined my exterior activity, He found in it not a single step, gesture or attitude that was not in the service of His love: I alone realized to the letter the Apostle's exhortation, "Whether you eat or drink, or whatever you do, do all for the glory of God."[3]

The extent of my love was equaled only by *its intensity.* I am preeminently the mystical Rose, not only because all my branches have borne their flower, but also because I have breathed out a fragrance so penetrating and so sweet that the whole earth, despite its stench of sin, was deliciously perfumed by it, even so far as to exert an irresistible attraction on the Word: "And the Word became flesh, and dwelt among us."[4]

Our supernatural love is but an irradiation of the uncreated love dwelling in the soul. "The love of God," says the Apostle, "has been poured into our hearts by the Holy Spirit who has been given to us."[5] And just as the resplendence of a crystal is measured both by the degree of its own transparency and the degree of light it receives, so this irradiation of divine love depends at the same time on our personal dispositions and the influx of the Sun of justice.

Now the souls of the other saints were never wholly free of those venial sins, imperfections and unruly inclinations which constitute so many opaque points.

By contrast, in my immaculate soul there is perfect transparency: nothing prevents it from receiving and appropriating all the rays that uncreated Love beams on it.

[3] *1 Cor.* 10:31.
[4] *John* 1:14.
[5] *Rom.* 5:5.

Moreover, it has pleased God to confer on me an incomparable measure of love. Because from the first moment of my conception He wants to love me more than the angels and saints together, He gives me a measure of grace which makes me more lovable in His eyes than all of them. And also, because He wants to be more loved by me alone than He is by all the angels and saints, He gives me a measure of charity which makes me more loving than all of them together.

Throughout my life He was pleased to put into play at every moment that capacity for loving. Sometimes He made use of the mirror of creatures to remind me of His beauty and His goodness. But most often He came Himself to fan the flame of love that burned in my heart.

A great Doctor, St. John of the Cross, teaches that "if the soul were to glimpse the least ray of God's beauty, it would be happy to suffer a thousand cruel deaths in order to enjoy a single instant of that beauty."[6] Indeed, because it has glimpsed that ray, the soul of the psalmist cries, "What have I in heaven, and besides You what do I desire upon earth? ... As the hind longs for the running waters, so my soul longs for You, O God ... When shall I go and behold the face of God?"[7] Similarly the soul of Teresa: "O life, life, where can you find your sustenance when you are absent from your Life? ... I die because I do not die!"[8]

If they felt so strongly, you may judge how forcefully and how completely my soul, incomparably more clearsighted and

[6] *Maxim* 164.
[7] *Psalms* 72:25 and 41:2,3.
[8] *Exclamations of the Soul to God,* #1, translated by E. Allison Peers in *The Complete Works of St. Teresa of Jesus* (New York: Sheed & Ward, 1953), vol. 2, p. 402; *Poems,* #1, in vol. 3, p. 277.

more loving than all the mystics together, must have cast itself into the arms of its sovereign Good every time He revealed to it a new ray of His infinite beauty.

And just as iron glows with an ever increasing heat in the measure in which the fire makes it more incandescent, so throughout my earthly life my heart sent up to God a flame of love more ardent every moment, because the Holy Spirit was always inflaming it further.

Finally, I was preeminently the mystical Rose because of *the continuity of my love.*

In the other saints charity is merely an inactive germ until the dawn of their reason; then it is a bud that opens only by degrees and breathes forth its perfume only at the hours when it is warmed by the rays of actual grace.

The rose of my love unfolded in the first hour. Surely if Jesus was in such haste to make Himself known and loved by Therese of Lisieux, who refused Him nothing from the age of three years, or by John the Baptist, to whom He revealed Himself at my visit to Elizabeth, you may imagine that He was still more impatient to make Himself known and loved by His own Mother.

Subsequently, in the whole course of my mortal life never for a single moment was any earthly concern able to distract my mind from the contemplation of infinite Beauty; never for a single moment could any earthly affection pry my heart loose from the infinite Good; never could any trial prevent my soul from saying with full assurance, "My Beloved is mine and I am His."[9]

However pale may be this sketch of the mystical Rose,

[9] *Cant.* 2:16.

promise yourself, my child, to place it often before your eyes, that its charm may pull you away gently from love of the world and of yourself; to pray often to the Rose, that its incomparable fragrance may penetrate your charity; to offer the mystical Rose often to Jesus, especially during your thanksgiving, to make up for the paltriness of your love.

TOWER OF DAVID

MARY, OUR PROTECTOR

I N comparing me to the tower of David the litany reminds you that you can find in my motherly protection an inviolable refuge against the three great enemies of your soul: the flesh, the world, the devil.

You hardly even fear *the devil,* because he does not attack you openly. Yet the Holy Spirit warns you that he is an obstinate enemy, repulsed by no defeat: "I will return to the dwelling from which I was driven out";[1] an implacable enemy, who seeks not only to despoil you but to devour you: "Your adversary the devil prowls about like a roaring lion, looking for someone to devour";[2] an enemy stronger than you, because after his fall he retains the powers of the angelic nature: "Our wrestling is not against flesh and blood, but ... against the spiritual forces of wickedness."[3]

By himself alone the devil can do you a great deal of harm: trouble your senses, obsess your imagination, seduce your

[1] *Luke* 11:24.
[2] *1 Pet.* 5:8.
[3] *Eph.* 6:12.

150

emotions, and thus falsify the judgments of your mind and mislead the choice of your will. He can harm you still more through his two accomplices, the flesh and the world, two "powers of darkness"[4] of which he is uncontested prince. When he so chooses, he launches their assault on your soul with consummate strategy.

The flesh is nothing but your seven unruly tendencies or capital sins. The Apostle shows you the flesh as the great antagonist of your spiritual life: "The flesh lusts against the spirit, and the spirit against the flesh";[5] an uncompromising antagonist: "It is not subject to the law of God, nor can it be";[6] a fierce antagonist, who aims at nothing less than death: "If you live according to the flesh you will die!"[7]

Truly, by the fever they arouse in your senses and the unwholesome dreams or recollections with which they obsess your memory, the seven evil inclinations labor without respite to obscure the vision of your conscience and point your will towards evil.

In this work of obfuscation and perversion they are powerfully aided by *the world*: that multitude of men who make happiness consist precisely in the satisfaction of the evil desires.[8]

At every moment, by its examples, its fashions, its amusements, the world tends to arouse one or another of your concupiscences. And what is worse, it tends to justify them by its false maxims, its false philosophies, its false doctrines, or merely by the imposing number of its votaries.

[4] *Col.* 1:13.
[5] *Gal.* 5:17.
[6] *Rom.* 8:7.
[7] *Rom.* 8:13.
[8] *1 John* 2:16.

Truly the world creates around your souls a poisoned atmosphere which, thanks to the present means of diffusion (press, motion pictures, radio), penetrates even into the most remote rural communities, the best guarded homes, the least sophisticated minds.

Such are the three enemies which keep working together to plunge you into the frightful abyss of mortal sin, and from there into the still more frightful abyss of eternal damnation. And it is certain that they would infallibly succeed if you were left to your own resources. Even the saints, says the Council of Orange, must always implore God's help to reach a good end.[9]

True for Christians of all times, this is still more true for those of today. To be sure, in the face of the dangers threatening them the sons of Adam have always been like little children, ignorant and improvident, never suspecting danger; imprudent and rash, enjoying the thrill of walking on the edge of a cliff. That is why God entrusts them to my motherly care. But it must be added that *the Christian of today* (as a result of the weakening of the faith) is less docile to the Church's prohibitions against the occasions of sin: dangerous books, spectacles, amusements; and also less courageous after being pardoned, to correct through penance the evil tendencies aroused in him by sin. It is in these unfavorable conditions, therefore, wounds unhealed, shackles still hindering, that he must face new battles.

Since you are at the same time more strongly attacked and less well armed, you are doubly in need of *assuring yourself*

[9] Denzinger-Bannwart-Umberg, *Enchiridion Symbolorum* (Freiburg: Herder & Co., 1937), #183, p. 88.

of my motherly protection, which you experience in two ways.

Sometimes I put you out of range of your enemies' blows, either by surrounding you with the protective barriers of a Christian family, education and environment, or by preventing the world and the devil from setting traps too dangerous for you. In heaven you will be touched with gratitude when you see the number of perils from which I thus preserved you.

Sometimes I let your adversaries multiply their attacks on you, but I give you the means of repelling them by clothing you beforehand with the spiritual armor of which the Apostle speaks.

As "Mother of knowledge"[10] I clothe you with the shield of the faith. Viewed by the senses, temptation appears as a pleasure; viewed by reason, as an advantage. In the eyes of faith it is nothing but a gross allurement hiding a deadly poison, a bargain as ignominious as it is unprofitable, since it proposes that you exchange heaven for hell, your title of God's son for that of devil's slave.

As "Mother of fair love"[11] I clothe you with the breastplate of charity. The soul enflamed with a great love sustains the spiritual combat more easily; for in all the allurements of the flesh, the world and the devil it sees only vile rubbish. It acts more effectively too; for, not content with avoiding serious offenses against its Beloved, it seeks to avoid the least infidelities; not content to cut off just a certain amount of the poisonous shoots of the seven capital sins, it attacks their very root.

[10] *Ecclus.* 24:24; Epistle of the Motherhood of the Blessed Virgin Mary.
[11] *Ibid.*

In short, my protection is a doubly enclosed fortress for you. On the outside my queenly power terrifies and discourages your enemies. On the inside my mother love shelters you tenderly under its wings besides arming you with all that is necessary for victory.

What must you do to assure yourself of a protection so desirable?

First, form the habit of looking to me and crying out to me at the first approach of danger. This looking towards the All-Pure will be an excellent distraction from the suggestions of the impure spirit; and this call for help will win you an increase of light to see temptation at its true value, an increase of strength to conquer it. If the temptation becomes nevertheless more and more insistent, you would come in spirit to find refuge in my arms, with absolute confidence that no enemy can reach you in that asylum.

Since you often forget to ask my protection in time of temptation, be sure to obtain it in advance by reciting the Memorare, the prayer "We fly to thy patronage" or a number of Hail Marys every day. I will inscribe every one of these appeals for help faithfully in my heart; and when the adversary pounces on you unexpectedly like a bird of prey, I will hasten to your aid, even if you do not think of praying to me.

Would you obtain a protection even more efficacious? Do not be afraid to ask for it. Strive to deserve it by an active devotion which will refuse neither service nor sacrifice, by an effective consecration which will entrust and deliver to me your whole being and all that you possess. Will I not redouble my solicitude to watch over that which is made doubly mine?

Promise me, then, my child, to neglect nothing that will assure you of my protection, repeating often with St. John Berchmans, "I shall not feel myself secure until I have acquired a true devotion to the Blessed Virgin."[12]

[12] *Documenta Vitae Spiritualis*, p. 58.

TOWER OF IVORY

MARY, MODEL OF MEEKNESS

THE tower by its solidity reminds you of my unshakable strength of soul. The tower of ivory, by the smoothness of its surface, reminds you that this strength is displayed gently. Such is the characteristic of an ideal strength of soul, the kind that enables us to impose our control and government not only on others but on ourselves.

By comparing your soul with mine you may learn, my child, how *perfect a model of meekness* I am, and how much you lack that quality yourself.

In the first place you have a tendency to be impatient with *the yoke of the faith* which God imposes on your mind; a tendency to break it by doubt and denial, or at least to shake it off by murmuring, by ignoring it in practice, by giving preference to the light of reason.

Convinced that human intelligence cannot embrace God's infinity, I never experienced either irritation or uneasiness in face of the unfathomable obscurity of His mysteries or His designs, even when they wounded my heart, as they did at the

156

time of Simeon's prophecy, the loss of the child Jesus, the drama of Calvary.

Convinced likewise that the least statement of God carries more weight than all our rational evidence, as soon as I read in the Scriptures, "God has said it," my mind acquiesced immediately, without resistance or holding back and without desiring other proof, any more than a person would desire the light of a lamp when he has that of the sun.

You are still more inclined to be impatient with *the yoke of the law,* to greet it with bad grace, bear it with ill humor and seek restlessly some pretext for lightening it or throwing it off.

In the meekness and humility of my heart I always considered the law a great justice and at the same time a great mercy. In the close network of the Mosaic ordinances that crisscrossed the whole course of my day, I saw only the hand of the sovereign Master directing His servant, the hand of the tenderest of fathers supporting the uncertain steps of His child.

Thus, far from raising the least complaint or criticism against the Mosaic ordinances, I submitted to all of them with docility, love and joy, even when human rulers imposed them on me harshly and indiscriminately; for they furnished me thus with an occasion of giving my heavenly Master and Father a more meritorious evidence of respect and love.

You are particularly inclined to be impatient and irritated with *the yoke of the cross.* You see it approach with great anxiety; you submit to it with repugnance; you drag rather than carry it, and you give yourself no rest until you have succeeded in getting rid of it.

By contrast, I welcomed and bore with unchanging meekness all the trials, great or small, which were the divinely erected landmarks of my earthly life.

It was not enough to refrain from murmuring when faced with each of those trials, to refrain from seeking compensations, resisting or escaping. I submitted to them promptly, gratefully, with love.

The reason is that in each of them I saw a bit of the cross of Jesus, and in consenting to them with my whole soul I was sure of giving Him great pleasure, collaborating in His redemptive work, acquiring an incalculable treasure of grace for souls and merit for myself!

If you find it hard to practice meekness towards God when He lays His threefold yoke on you, you find it still harder to practice *meekness towards your neighbor* whenever he inflicts the least injury on you. Your offended self love reacts then by displeasure, antipathy, anger and sometimes outward reprisals: giving back criticism for criticism, injury for injury, blow for blow!

No one ever sees a limb taking revenge, becoming irritated or impatient, or even complaining against another limb, awkward or infirm, which causes it annoyance and suffering. On the contrary, it has a motive for surrounding the other member with more solicitude, compassion and tenderness.

That is the exact image of the unfailing kindness I practiced toward those who were a burden on me: my neighbors who would entertain me with their pointless concerns when my mind was wholly occupied with God and the things of God; my relatives who often responded to my thoughtful attentions only with indifference or rudeness; my compatriots, obtuse and jealous, who treated my divine Son as insane; the disciples, so inclined to lack consideration for Him and so slow to believe in His word; those scribes and Pharisees who were intent on discrediting His message and hindering His work by the most hateful methods; all those wretches who covered Him with blows and spittle before Caiphas, treated Him as a fool before Herod, scourged Him and crowned Him with thorns before Pilate, crucified Him and mocked at His agony on Calvary!

In a like situation you would not have failed to call down the most terrible revenge on those criminals, to ask that fire from heaven consume them or the earth swallow them up!

For my part, my only concern then was to imitate the indescribable meekness of Jesus. He made no move to turn His face away from the blows and spittle:[1] I did not let myself make any move to save Him from the whips, the thorns or the nails! As a lamb led to the slaughter, He did not open His mouth to complain:[2] I refrained from expressing either curse or reproach or lamentation; and if in my heart I appealed to the sovereign Judge, it was only to ask His pardon for my tormentors: "Father, forgive them, for they do not know what they are doing!"[3]

Along with meekness towards God and neighbor, learn *meekness toward yourself* also in my school.

Are you troubled by the fever of desire: a desire to free yourself from an evil or to obtain a good? Consider with what serene patience I waited for God to put an end to Joseph's cruel anxiety, which oppressed me as much as it did him;

[1] *Is.* 50:6.
[2] *Is.* 53:7.
[3] *Luke* 23:34.

with what patience also I awaited after the Ascension the longed-for hour which was to reunite me with Jesus, my Life and my All.

Are you troubled by the fever of uneasiness over an uncertain future or a dreaded reckoning? See with what peace (drawn from abandonment to God) I lived thirty-three years under the threat of the sword foretold by the aged Simeon.

Are you troubled by the fever of work? Consider with what grace and sweetness I gave myself to the service of Jesus, though there could not be a task more important and absorbing.

Does your trouble come from the vexation of failures, persistent miseries, repeated falls? You will quickly find peace by dissipating in the glow of my humility the self love that begets vexation.

And even if the trouble and disturbance comes principally from your irritable nerves, you will soon learn, by keeping your eyes fixed on me, to penetrate with calmness all the thoughts of your mind, all the affections of your heart, all the words of your lips and even the least movements of your body.

Yes, my child, by living intimately with me you will experience an ardent desire to take on the threefold meekness I have made you admire in me. You will obtain the grace by praying much to me; for, as St. John of the Cross teaches, if Jesus does not soften the soul by His grace, it will persist forever in its natural hardness.[4] You should love to repeat to me often, therefore, with the Church:

[4] *Maxim* 28; in *The Complete Works of St. John of the Cross*, vol. 3, p. 244.

"Virgo singularis,
Inter omnes mitis,
Nos, culpis solutos,
Mites fac et castos."[5]

[5] Hymn *Ave Maris Stella*: "O incomparable Virgin, meek above all others, make us, freed from sin, meek and chaste"; literal translation by Dom Matthew Britt, O.S.B., in *The Hymns of the Breviary and Missal* (New York: Benziger Brothers, Inc., 1952), p. 348.

HOUSE OF GOLD

MARY AND THE LOVE OF NEIGHBOR

GOLD is the symbol of charity. I am all charity. To God and to neighbor I have given only love.[1] In explaining my title of mystical Rose I showed you, my child, how I am a perfect model of charity towards God. I am going to teach you how I am a perfect model of charity toward neighbor.

To love one's neighbor is to be ready to *pardon his offenses,* even the most serious and inexcusable.

Herod sought to kill my gentle Son in His infancy. The Pharisees kept pursuing Him during His public life with their calumnies and snares. During His Passion I saw Judas betray Him, the disciples abandon Him, the people prefer Barabbas to Him, the executioners scourge Him, crown Him with thorns and nail Him to the cross. And because of the unique love that united me to Jesus and identified me with Him, I felt these insults and sufferings more keenly than if they had been inflicted on myself.

[1] St. Therese of Lisieux, *The Story of a Soul,* translated by the Rev. Michael Day, Cong. Orat. (Westminster, Md.: The Newman Press, 1954), ch. 11, p. 192.

Yet instead of conceiving the least hatred or vengeance against all those who were thus driving the sword relentlessly into my heart, my only thought was to call down divine mercy and indulgence on them, saying with Jesus, "Father, forgive them, for they do not know what they are doing."

And when the Apostles who had abandoned Him returned to me, Peter who had denied Him three times, and later those converts of Pentecost day who had demanded His death; following the example of the father in the parable, I granted them all an immediate pardon, requiring no long entreaty or prior reparation; a generous pardon, refraining from any reproach or even any illusion to their offense; a heartfelt pardon, letting it be understood that everything was forgotten once and for all.

To love one's neighbor is to *put up with his defects* and weaknesses *untiringly.*

Gifted with a delicate sensibility, as Virgin and Immaculate, I could not but feel keenly the injuries of a coarse, sensual environment.

Following the Apostle's advice, I put up with all these affronts with patience, keeping my lips from all complaint, my mind from all blame, my heart from all bitterness; with humility, judging that I was already granted more consideration and attention than I deserved: a mere creature, being nothing by herself, has no right to anything; finally, with meekness, with that unchanging gentleness of the healthy member who suffers all from the sick member and does not make him suffer anything.

To love one's neighbor is to *sympathize with his ills,* spiritual or temporal.

My immaculate heart, not being hardened like yours by the many forms of selfishness, showed itself ready to feel and to comfort the least distress. Consider how I intervened at Cana to spare the wedding couple a little embarrassment and confusion.

I had even more reason, following the example of Jesus, to be readily moved to pity over more serious distress: the leper's ulcerated body, the blind man's sightless eyes, the widow's desolation as she mourned her only son; above all, the misery of souls, soiled by sin, enslaved to base desires, tyrannized by Satan who pushes them blindfolded toward the abyss.

And to help them effectively I consented, as did Jesus, to a life of poverty, humility, sacrifice and finally the unspeakable agony of Calvary, which for me was a hundred times worse than death. There is no greater compassion than to lay down one's own life to save others' lives. To rescue you from eternal death I laid down more than my life by consenting to the immolation of Jesus.

To love one's neighbor is to *esteem and respect him.*

Enlightened by a vivid faith, I always discerned and respected in my neighbor his character of servant and child of God, always worthy of esteem and respect, even when he had fallen into the mire.

Thus, far from passing unjust, rash or overly severe judgments on him, I was inclined to look for something to excuse his intentions if not his actions. Far from investigating and publicizing something that could injure his reputation, I was eager and glad to discover and point out what redounded to his honor. Far from making him feel his inferiority or his failure, I showed him all the respect proper to his rank, not those attentions which proceed from affectation and tend above all to show off their author, but those which proceed from, and show, true regard.

To love one's neighbor is to *wish him well,* to care for his interests and himself.

I had the interests of my neighbors at heart as my own, rejoicing sincerely at their gains, their virtues, their successes, grieving no less sincerely over their reverses, their spiritual or temporal misfortunes.

With regard to their person, however repulsive it might be, I never entertained those feelings of aversion or antipathy which are betrayed by an air of coolness, a curt reply, disagreeable behavior, the desire to flee their presence, their conversation, their attentions.

On the contrary, I always showed a heartfelt sympathy, letting my neighbors know by a welcoming expression, friendly words and thoughtful attentions whenever we met that I was happy to find myself in their company and desirous of giving them as much pleasure and benefit as I could.

For, as my little Therese justly observes, good will towards our brethren must not remain shut up in the heart, under a bushel, but must appear outside, on a candlestick, to gladden all those who are in the house.[2]

Finally, since good will must blossom out in good deeds, to love one's neighbor is to *do him as much good as one can.*

By depriving myself of superfluities and sometimes of necessities, I made an alms of my possessions to those poorer than I.

[2] *Ibid.,* ch. 9, p. 146.

To all, poor or rich, I gave the alms of my services, without counting the cost.

And I always practiced this service with the intentions recommended by Jesus: not through self interest, to assure myself of another's services; not through vanity, to draw recognition and praise to myself; but through pure love of God, whom I was happy to serve in the person of His children.

I practiced it also with the dispositions recommended by Jesus, that is to say with that courtesy which encourages the petitioner, that kindness which anticipates his desires, that generosity which spares neither time nor trouble, that eagerness which removes any fear of being a burden, that delicacy which hides the price of the service rendered. And if duty or circumstance obliged me to say no, I said it so graciously that my refusal gave as much pleasure as an acceptance.

Finally, to all men without exception I gave, abundantly and constantly, the alms of my prayers, satisfactions and merits, looking forward to giving them, at the foot of the cross, the supreme alms of the blood and sacrifice of Jesus!

Never grow tired, my child, of contemplating the perfect example of charity I gave you throughout my life, nor of asking me for all the graces necessary to bring you as close as possible to that desired ideal. When occasion offers, strive to practice patience, pardon, compassion, service, as you think I would practice them in your place.

If you follow these counsels faithfully, you will soon come into possession of the blessedness promised charitable souls: the happiness of feeling yourself daily more like Jesus, of fulfilling that one of His precepts which He has most at heart, of being adjusted to the most imperious impulse of

His grace, which tends to unite the members of His mystical body intimately to one another; the happiness of knowing that your love for God is authentic and on the way to becoming perfect, as the Apostle assures you: "If we love one another, God abides in us and His love is perfected in us."[3]

[3] *1 John* 4:12.

ARK OF THE COVENANT

MARY AS HELPER

I N their journeying toward the promised land Israel had received the ark of the covenant as a visible pledge of the divine power and goodness which were to help them overcome all obstacles: the sands and mirages of the desert, the flood waters of the Jordan, the walls of Jericho. God gives me the mission of accompanying you throughout your exile as the pledge and the agent of His infinite power and goodness, to help you get over the various obstacles that bar your way to the heavenly country.

The first obstacle, apt to arise at every turn, is *the mirage of temptations* that urge you to give up the pursuit of eternal happiness and cling to short-lived, false joys.

Here I have two ways of coming to the aid of my faithful servants.

Sometimes, using the queenly power which enables me to act on the hearts of men and the course of events, I simply suppress the temptations, at least those which I consider too formidable for your weakness. To repay you for having

entrusted yourselves to me with the humility and wholehearted-
ness of a little child aware of his helplessness and looking to
his mother for everything, I treat you as little children, removing with motherly care all the traps that the world and
the devil are setting for you.

To furnish an occasion for greater merit, God may require
that you be tried by more dangerous temptations. Using my
power as Mediatrix, I obtain graces of light to show you how
base and deceitful the tempter's allurement is, graces of
strength to enable you to tear yourselves away from the fascination of the most disturbing pleasures and to confront the
most frightening sufferings and humiliations.

But this presupposes ordinarily that by your zeal in praying
to me you make it easy for me to obtain choice graces for
you, and that by your zeal in imitating me you make it easy
for yourselves to correspond to those graces.

To overcome a grave temptation is to take a great step
forward on the way to heaven; to succumb to the temptation
is to leave that road and *fall into the abyss of mortal sin.* As
long as it lies in that abyss the soul cannot earn any merit
for heaven; and if it has not succeeded in getting out before
the moment of death, it will become the hopeless prey of
hell.

As Advocate and Refuge of sinners I have the power of
freeing those unfortunates from the prison of sin and reopening
the way to heaven for them; but here again, the more faithful they are in imploring my intervention, the easier it is for
me to help them.

Some, determined to persevere in their sinful habits, address their prayers to me simply to be freed from an incon-

venient remorse or to be assured a sort of impunity. Obviously such devotion is nothing but an illusion and a lie, since it is wholly vitiated by their bad intention.

Others have not yet decided to break away from their bad habits; but, like spoiled children who do not love their mother enough to obey her in everything but do love her enough to do something for her on occasion, they are faithful in offering me daily, with the right intention, the homage of some pious practice. This evidence of trust and affection, however slight it be, may allow me to obtain for them the grace of conversion, as I did for the suicide of whom the Curé of Ars said, "He is saved. Between the parapet and the water he made an act of contrition!"[1] Still this remains a very uncertain pledge of salvation, and becomes more uncertain the longer one delays in opening the heart freely to the first harbinger of infinite Mercy, the desire for conversion.

A last group have already welcomed that desire, and they even make sincere efforts to resist temptations; but, weakened by long habit, they fall so often and so heavily that they almost despair of victory. To them I give the assurance of complete and final victory over their bad habits if they persevere in their efforts and in devotion to me at the same time. But the devotion must be stubbornly trustful, and as humble and urgent as they feel themselves to be weak.

Always in danger throughout your life, your perseverance is exposed to still graver perils when you have to *cross the formidable river of death* which separates time and eternity. For, when your soul is more weakened by the sufferings of the body and more disturbed by the anxiety of the final separa-

[1] Abbé Francis Trochu, *Intuitions du Curé d'Ars,* vol. 1, p. 23.

tion, the devil redoubles his trickery and his fury against it, knowing that this is the decisive battle.[2]

It is also the moment when I redouble my solicitude, to protect and assist all the redeemed, but especially those who have shown some devotion to me.

Most of them have been satisfied to honor me as their Protector by asking me every day to relieve the distress of the present moment and the more terrifying distress of the moment of death: "Pray for us now and at the hour of our death!"

I have gathered up every "pray for us" addressed to me throughout their earthly pilgrimage and faithfully kept all in my heart. And now that the decisive hour has struck, I take them out, all perfumed with my purity and aglow with my love, to offer them to God in the name of those departing souls as so many acts of reparation to disarm His justice, so many supplications to obtain from His mercy the supreme grace of final perseverance.

Others, unfortunately too few, have not stopped at asking my protection; they have loved me tenderly as their all-good Mother, served me faithfully as their all-lovable Queen, striven to imitate me as the most perfect and inspiring of models. And thus they have deserved that I obtain for them not only a holy death but a sweet one.

Faithful to the appointment they have made with me so many times during their life, "pray for us ... at the hour of our death," I enter the lists where they are fighting the last fight alone. If they are troubled by the remembrance of their sins and the approach of the sovereign Judge, I reassure

[2] Council of Trent; Denzinger-Bannwart-Umberg, *Enchiridion Symbolorum,* #907, p. 321.

them by reminding them of the infinite Mercy whose living image I am. If they are terrified by Satan, who takes his revenge for not being able to conquer them by tormenting them with thoughts of horror or dread, I surround them with my tenderness as with an impregnable enclosure in which they feel perfectly secure. If they are burdened with their last sufferings and all but crushed under the weight of their failing body, I either soften their pangs notably or obtain for them the strength to bear with the pain patiently and trustingly, so as to transform their last hour into a true sacrifice, capable of atoning for other souls and greatly embellishing their own crown.

To those for whom I have procured the grace of a good death, a last obstacle, like an insurmountable wall, may forbid immediate entrance into the promised land: *the obligation to undergo in purgatory the temporal punishment* they have neglected to make up in this life.

Although they acquiesce with love in this sentence of expiation, the souls in purgatory suffer cruelly to feel themselves detained in that exile and those torments, far from the blessed country, the infinite Goodness and Beauty to which they tend with all the energies of their being, now that they are free from all earthly attachment.

Great Doctors and the Church herself in her liturgy teach you that I can intervene ("beata Maria semper Virgine intercedente")[3] to soften or shorten their terrible ordeal.

First I incite my children on earth to offer for the souls in purgatory both their personal works of reparation and the

[3] Daily Mass for the Dead, 2nd collect.

satisfactions of Christ generously placed at their disposal by indulgences and especially by the Mass.

Then, since your prayers and sacrifices on behalf of the deceased have little value in God's eyes because He sees them issuing from a heart poorly cleansed and not very fervent, I confer a great value on them by offering them myself, with my immaculate, motherly heart, wholly pleasing to God.

Finally I intervene through my prayer, to which God always listens, to dispose Him to accept the ransom offered by the faithful on earth for those in purgatory; for, however excellent may be the satisfactions offered by the Church militant, God has not promised by any means to let the prisoners of His justice in the Church suffering reap benefit from them.

Thus the elect have me to thank for all the graces which have insured or hastened their admission into heaven.

What could be more desirable, my child, than constant victory over temptations, a sweet, holy death and prompt liberation from purgatory? Form the habit of praying to me, loving and serving me more every day, and I will surely obtain for you these three great graces which will open a sure and easy way past the worst obstacles to the heavenly fatherland.

GATE OF HEAVEN

DEVOTION TO MARY A PLEDGE OF SALVATION

I N the opinion of a great number of saints, my child, devotion to me is *a sign and a pledge of predestination.*

Thus, in the East, St. John Damascene addresses these words to me: "My Sovereign, receive the prayer of your servant, a sinner indeed, but one who loves you ardently . . . and looks on you as the certain pledge of his salvation."[1] And St. Germanus of Constantinople adds, in substance, that devotion to me is a sign and cause of supernatural life in a soul, as breathing is a sign and cause of natural life in a body.[2]

In the West, witnesses for this belief include: St. Anselm: "Most Blessed Virgin, it is impossible that anyone should perish who turns to you and upon whom you look!"[3] St. Catherine of Siena: "No man who takes refuge with Mary can ever become the prey of hell."[4] St. Lawrence Justinian:

[1] *Homilia 6, in Nativitatem B. Virginis Mariae,* #12; in *P. G.,* vol. 96, col. 680.

[2] *Concio in S. Mariae Zonam;* in *P. G.,* vol. 98, col. 377.

[3] *Oratio 52, ad S. Virginem Mariam;* in *P. L.,* vol. 158, col. 956.

[4] *Dialogue,* ch. 139.

"No one devoted to Mary will be excluded from the presence of God."[5] St. Alphonsus de Liguori: "It is impossible for a client of Mary, who is faithful in honoring and recommending himself to her, to be lost."[6]

The liturgy for its part places these words of Wisdom on my lips: "Blessed is the man who hears me, and who watches daily at the entrance of my house. He who finds me shall find life, and shall have salvation from the Lord!"[7] And elsewhere: "He who listens to me shall not be confounded . . . those who glorify me shall have life everlasting."[8]

Thus in the opinion of the saints and of the liturgy, to show great devotion to me is to insure oneself against the risks of damnation and to provide for oneself a real guarantee of salvation.

How can devotion to me procure this all-important benefit for you?

Final perseverance or salvation (for it is all one) is presented to you by Christ as the *prize for a victory* over the flesh, the world and the devil, who are constantly allied to drag you into the abyss. I have shown you elsewhere (Tower of David) how I protect you effectively against these three formidable enemies of your salvation.

Final perseverance is presented to you again as a *splendid salary* which God assigns to those who glorify Him by ob-

[5] *De Triumphali Agone Christi,* ch. 18; in *Opera Omnia* (Venice: de Albertis, 1606), leaf 213, verso.

[6] *The Glories of Mary,* translation edited by the Rev. Eugene Grimm, C.SS.R. (Brooklyn: Redemptorist Fathers, 1931), part 1, ch. 8, p. 220.

[7] *Prov.* 8:34-35; Epistle of the Nativity of the Blessed Virgin Mary.

[8] *Ecclus.* 24:30,31; Epistle of the Motherhood of the Blessed Virgin Mary.

serving His commandments, fulfilling His will. As Treasurer and Dispenser of graces I keep offering you, despite your incurable unworthiness, all the inspiration and help you could want, to discern, accept and execute the divine will even in its hardest requirements.

Above all, final perseverance is presented to you as *a gift* which must be obtained by prayer, for it is too precious to be bought by way of merit for an equitable price. "Continual prayer," says St. Thomas Aquinas, "is necessary for man that he may enter heaven."[9] And St. Alphonsus de Liguori adds: "He who prays is certainly saved. He who prays not is certainly damned."[10]

But just any kind of prayer is not enough. God asks of you a *persevering* prayer, that you may adequately honor and appreciate this priceless gift; a *humble* prayer, that you may render homage to His infinite grandeur and holiness; a *trusting* prayer, that you may give homage to His fatherly goodness and tenderness, equally infinite.

It is the characteristic of devotion to me that it makes such supplication easy and almost spontaneous for you.

It makes *perseverance* easy: it is a pleasure and not a hardship for a little child to converse with his mother and repeat to her untiringly what is in his heart, especially if the thing in question is his worst fear or his highest hope. Yes, whereas you find it hard to ask God three times in succession for the same favor, you experience no difficulty in asking me

[9] *Summa Theologica,* IIIa, q. 39, a. 5.
[10] *The Great Means of Salvation and of Perfection,* translation edited by the Rev. Eugene Grimm, C.SS.R. (Brooklyn: Redemptorist Fathers, 1927), ch. 1, p. 49.

fifty times in succession, in the rosary, for the grace of a good death: "and at the hour of our death."

Devotion to me makes *humility* easy: "Indeed I tell you, unless you turn back and become like the little children, you shall by no means enter the kingdom of heaven."[11] If you have a truly filial love for me, you will find it quite natural to confide in me your needs and your sorrows, to show me your wounds and your stains, to confess to me your laxity and your sins; in a word, to behave towards me as a little child toward its mother. Experience proves that any other means, on the contrary, allows you only with great difficulty to place yourself, in spirit and in truth, in that attitude of a little child demanded by Christ.

Finally, devotion to me makes *trust* easy. "Let him ask with faith, without hesitation," says the Apostle St. James; one who hesitates should not "think that he will receive anything from the Lord."[12]

Often you dare not even pray to God. You are afraid to raise your soiled hands to infinite Holiness, your guilty hands to infinite Justice. It does not bother you, however, to turn to me, in whom you see only a Mother, and a Mother of mercy, having only the mission of helping you, not that of judging you.

More often you do dare to pray to God, but you dare not believe firmly in the efficacy of your prayer.

To be sure, it is quite true that neither the value of your supplication, deficient in so many ways, nor the influence of your person, so far from agreeable to God, is apt to touch infinite Mercy, still less to disarm infinite Justice.

[11] *Matt.* 18:3.　　　[12] *James* 1:6,7.

But it is still more true that by lavishing on me the evidences of a true devotion you are making it possible and easy for me to intervene on your behalf; for that intervention itself is a signal grace which as a rule must be desired and implored: "Ask and you shall receive."

Now since God is most highly pleased both by my prayer and by my person, I have great influence to draw out His mercy and disarm His justice.

And thereby I obtain for you, besides the ordinary graces, an abundance of choice graces, of which you are doubly unworthy but which are nevertheless practically indispensable in your weakness to lead you back to the way of salvation or keep you in it to the end.

It is especially through her model prayer, "Holy Mary, Mother of God, pray for us sinners now and at the hour of our death," that the Church makes you implore the supreme grace of final perseverance. That prayer is most fitted to inspiring these three fundamental dispositions.

It places you in a position of trusting by making you implore her who wants to assure your salvation and can do it: "Holy Mary": the true Mother of your soul, supremely loving, compassionate and devoted, supremely desirous of preserving for you the supernatural life she has given you; "Mother of God": she who, having a right to all her Son's gratitude and love, has supreme influence with Him to obtain any grace or pardon whatsoever.

This prayer puts you in a position of humility by recalling that you are a "sinner": a culprit, who has committed the supreme injustice and ingratitude of insulting his Creator and Father; a wretch, groveling in the dust of venial sin or the mud of mortal sin and consumed by the leprosy of the seven evil inclinations.

Finally, through the unceasing repetition of the "pray for us" in the rosary or the litany, you are made to imitate the perseverance of the shipwrecked man who keeps crying for help until someone has rescued him from the deep.

Since devotion to me is a pledge of salvation, resolve, my child, to root it ever deeper in your heart, believing that the truer and deeper it is, the surer will the pledge be.

Yes, the more you pray to me with humility, trust and perseverance, the greater ease will I have in obtaining for you those choice graces which insure a good death. The more you apply yourself to imitating me, the more ease will you have yourself in corresponding to those graces. Finally, the more you increase in love of me, the more I shall have it at heart (for "I love those who love me")[13] not only to make you reach heaven but to let you have a preferred place near me.

[13] *Prov.* 8:17; Common of feasts of the Blessed Virgin Mary, 1st nocturn, 1st lesson.

MORNING STAR

*DEVOTION TO MARY A REMEDY AGAINST
SADNESS*

Every evil that afflicts your body, mind, or heart, my
child, plunges you into *sadness;* the feverish desire to be
freed from that evil plunges you into *restlessness.*

Far from lessening your ordeal, both of these emotions
can only aggravate it; and moreover they constitute a serious
danger for your soul, by giving it a distaste for piety and
virtue and by making it more vulnerable to the many temptations the devil is sure to raise against it in these hours of
crisis. "There is no profit in sadness," says the Holy Spirit.[1]

It is important, therefore, that you free yourself promptly
from the clutches of sadness and disquiet. Now just as the
morning star thins out the darkness of the night and announces
its approaching disappearance, so *I have the mission and the
power of dissipating that sadness* and restlessness which come
sometimes to envelop your soul like a dark night. And that

[1] *Ecclus.* 30:25.

180

is why the saints are pleased to give me the gracious name of morning Star.

A first group of sad and restless moods is caused principally by *too excitable nerves,* too vivid sensibilities, too lively an imagination. Without neglecting a sensible hygiene which will attack the evil at its root, you will seek some diversion as an immediate remedy.

And there is no better diversion to withdraw you from the obsession of that more or less unhealthy sadness or restlessness than to look on me, to cry out to me, following St. Bernard's advice, "Look up at the Star, call upon Mary."[2]

Your mind is beset by gloomy, foreboding ideas. I am all splendor and light, beauty and enticement.

Your heart is plunged in floods of bitterness. I am "meek above all others,"[3] "sweetness itself,"[4] as the liturgy sings.

Your will is crushed by the feeling of its impotence in face of real or imaginary difficulties, impossible to foresee or to surmount. Am I not a most discerning Mother, to learn your true needs or dangers; an all-good Mother, to sympathize with them; an all-powerful Mother, to provide for them?

Yes, to look on me and remember me is to introduce into the soul a ray of light that consoles, pacifies and reassures it.

But St. Bernard does not stop at telling you to "think of Mary"; he adds, "Call upon Mary." And the Church herself invites you to send up your cries and your sighs to me when you feel that this earth is changed into a valley of tears: "To

[2] *Second Sermon on the Glories of the Virgin Mother,* #17; in *P. L.,* vol. 183, col. 70; in *St. Bernard's Sermons for the Seasons and Principal Festivals of the Year,* vol. 1, p. 92.

[3] Hymn *Ave Maris Stella.*

[4] Antiphon *Salve Regina.*

thee do we cry ... To thee do we send up our sighs ... in this valley of tears."[5] This supplication, ardent and repeated, will permit me to obtain for you graces of light, which will show you clearly that some distracting thought or feverish concern is only a vain imagination. It will permit me also to obtain graces of strength which will enable you to master your sensibilities and your imagination, to throw off those feelings of helplessness, anxiety and melancholy which hamper your prayer or the duties of your state and make you carry a heavy cross without any profit for earth or heaven.

A second group of sad and restless moods is nothing but *the bitter fruit of the various evil inclinations*: sadness of pride, which spends entire days brooding over the humiliation caused by a defeat, a blunder or a fault, by a jeer, a criticism, a mere oversight; sadness of envy, which grieves at seeing oneself outclassed by others; sadness of sensuality, obliged to undergo cold, heat, sickness, or some restriction in food, sleep or rest; sadness of poorly restrained impurity, which sees forbidden what it desires most; sadness of sloth, which rebels under the yoke of duty.

You must act vigorously against these various sad moods; for, not content with making you unhappy like the preceding ones, they aim directly at making you guilty, even dissimulating their dishonorable source in order to succeed better.

Here again, to look on me and cry out to me is the most effective means of unmasking them and putting them to flight. For you cannot long fix your eyes on me, so humble, pure, good and valiant, without becoming acutely aware and deep-

[5] *Ibid.*

ly ashamed of the pride, envy, lust and sloth that have given birth to sadness or restlessness.

Then, far from continuing to grieve at the blows received from those various evil desires, you will thank the Lord for them: "Thank You, my God, for having permitted this trial for my greater good." The evil sadness will be changed into a holy joy.

For my part, I will answer your supplications by obtaining choice graces for you, which will help you attack the roots of those seven desires of which the evil sadness is a poisonous offshoot.

The practice of looking to me and calling upon me is no less effective to combat the third kind of sad feelings, caused by the *various ordeals of Providence.*

Thus you are plunged into grief or disturbance because adverse times have reduced you (or are going to reduce you) to straitened circumstances and poverty; because a scandal or a calumny has soiled (or is going to soil) your reputation; because the death of a spouse or a child has just destroyed your earthly happiness; because sickness or old age is going to make you a burden to yourself and others.

In these unhappy situations do not grow tired of looking to me and crying out to me, pouring your trouble and anguish into my motherly heart; and you will be surprised to see how quickly I succeed in making your afflicted, troubled heart glow with peace and resignation, and even with that spiritual joy which the Apostle recommends to you in the worst ordeals: "Rejoice in the Lord always."[6]

At other times you are grieved and troubled because the

---

[6] *Phil.* 4:4.

flesh, the world and the devil have formed an alliance to besiege you with such violent temptations that you despair of
being able to cope with them for long. Look upon me, cry
out to me; come to huddle, figuratively, in my arms; and you
will find there the sweetest and surest of refuges, for what I
guard is well guarded!

Only, that your supplication may deserve to bring you into
that desirable shelter, it must be sincere and urgent, like the
distressed cry of one pursued, on the point of being caught
and devoured: "Save me from the lion's mouth!"; like the
cry of the shipwrecked man caught in the whirlpool: "Snatch
me from the deep!"[7]

Finally, you are troubled and grieved at the remembrance
of your past sins, unhappily quite grave and quite numerous.

This remembrance is beneficial if its effect is to keep you
in a state of habitual regret for your sins and a desire to keep
expiating them more and more. But if it tends to cast you
into a sterile depression and, what is worse, to make you
lapse into despair, that is the time, more than ever, to look
upon me and cry out to me.

Being the reflection and the servant of infinite Mercy, I
will quickly lead you to think about It, believe in It, entrust
yourself to It, by arousing in your heart these sentiments of
the little Therese: "Even if I had all the crimes possible on
my conscience, I am sure I should lose none of my confidence.
Heartbroken with repentance, I would simply throw myself
into my Savior's arms . . . and in the twinkling of an eye all
those thousands of sins would be consumed as a drop of water
cast into a blazing fire."[8]

[7] *Psalms* 21:22; 68:16.
[8] *The Story of a Soul,* ch. 10, p. 181.

Thus, my child, whatever may be the cause of your restlessness or sadness, be faithful in looking to me and crying out
to me, and my sweet image will hasten to brighten the night
of your soul like a radiant star dissipating your trouble or
affliction, allaying your fear and anguish.

"Look up at the Star, call upon Mary!"

HEALTH OF THE SICK

MARY, HEALER OF SOULS

W HEN you call upon me as Health of the Sick, my child, you think of the bodily cures I effect at Lourdes and at my other shrines.

Actually I am above all a healer of souls. God lets me heal bodies only by exception, in so far as this is necessary to maintain my children's faith and trust. On the other hand, He gives me the mission and the power to cure all the ailments of every soul that has recourse to me.

The first service I render your sick soul is to *reveal the existence and the gravity of its illness.* As long as it remains ignorant of these, it desires neither doctor nor medicine, and in vain does the Church have it say, "Lord, only say the word and I shall be healed."[1]

In what does the great malady of your soul consist? In its tendency, inborn or acquired, to covet pleasures, riches and honors without taking into account the restrictions or prohibitions imposed by God; in its tendency to seek in everything not what pleases God but what pleases vanity, greed, impurity, sensuality, revenge or laziness.

The presence in you of those seven sources of infection

[1] Ordinary of the Mass.

which are the seven capital sins causes you no distress or worry; yet they engender in your poor soul (as I am going to show you) the same disorders that the most serious maladies produce in the body.

Sickness takes away the appetite. See how indifferent your unruly tendencies make you towards eternal happiness and those banquets of grace—prayer, Mass, Communion—which alone provide the strength for climbing the rugged way to heaven.

Sickness takes away all taste and aptitude for work. See how sloth, sensuality and pride make you find spiritual duties difficult and repulsive: the various tasks of piety, penance or apostolate which God assigns to you.

Aggravated sickness leads successively to sluggishness and fever. Does not your unruly love of rest and ease often plunge you into a sort of lethargy that makes you insensitive to the needs, evils and perils of your poor soul! And does not the unruly love of success or pleasure provoke in you a ferment of thoughts and aspirations, an expenditure of energy as exhausting and at the same time as sterile as that of a fever?

Sickness makes your body suffer. Unruly tendencies make your soul suffer no less. How many gloomy moods have no other cause than wounded vanity, thwarted sensuality, laziness disturbed!

Moreover, those tendencies produce a particular weakness in each of your faculties. They make your mind a poor blind man whose feverish gaze can no longer perceive supernatural realities in their true outline. They make your will a poor weakling who despite all his efforts can neither overtake nor grasp what he desires most: grace, merit, virtues. They make your imagination and your senses poor fools, prey to the most illusive or distorted images and impressions.

Such, my child, are the truths which I keep placing before your eyes. What could be more effective in persuading you to have recourse to the divine Physician, who alone can cure your terrible spiritual ailments, but who wants to do so only in the measure in which you ask Him?

I persuade you to implore the grace of healing by disclosing the gravity of your sickness. *I help you obtain that grace* by making up for the insufficiency or the unworthiness of your prayer.

Your prayer does not deserve to be heard because it lacks perseverance and warmth. If you suffer in your body you feel constrained to cry out to God with all your strength as long as the sickness lasts. On the other hand, since you do not feel the ailments of the soul, you soon tire of imploring a cure, and moreover your prayer is often a perfunctory duty of the lips alone.

But I love your poor soul more than you love it yourself. I see clearly the abyss of evil and sin into which the unruly tendencies are plunging it. And I experience an ardent, constant desire for its cure. By your mandate I pray for your soul; and I do not fail to put that ardor and that insistence into my prayer.

Even when your prayer is perfect, you still have great need of my intercession.

To ask for the healing of a soul is to request a miracle greater than the healing of a body. And you serve the good God so poorly that you hardly have any claim to a favor so exceptional. Admit rather that you are positively unworthy of it; for this grace of healing which you implore has already been offered you thousands of times, especially at each Communion, and until now you have not appreciated it. That it may be offered you once more, I must disarm infinite Justice by throwing into the balance the whole weight of my satisfactions on Calvary.

Finally, *having obtained the medicine for you, I help you take it* despite its bitterness.

To heal the body you must first of all remove whatever favors the multiplication of the morbid germs. To heal your soul you must keep it jealously from everything that arouses or feeds its unruly tendencies: "If your eye is an occasion of sin to you, pluck it out and cast it from you."[2]

If you imposed a perpetual, rigorous fast on your evil tendencies, as you are invited to do by the grace I have obtained for you, there is no doubt that they would quickly be rendered weak and inoffensive.

But perseverance in that practice requires hatred of those inclinations; and you, on the contrary, cherish them tenderly as a part of yourself.

Now the easiest way, and at the same time the most effective, to succeed in hating them is to live close to me. Obviously, the more you live in the radiation of my purity, humility and charity, the more you will be inclined to develop a distaste and a horror for your inclinations to impurity, pride and selfishness; the more vigilant and unyielding you will be in not making the least concession to them.

But it is not enough to refrain from cultivating those morbid germs which are the unruly tendencies. They must be fought

[2] *Matt.* 18:9.

and, if possible, destroyed. By what means? By making your ardor in the quest for suffering, renunciation and humiliation equal to their insistence that you seek pleasures, riches and honors.

Unfortunately you have not the courage to apply this salutary but harsh treatment to yourself, nor to accept it patiently when God applies it to you by way of some ordeal.

Would you acquire that courage? Hasten to increase in love of me and devotion to me. See how the little one who really loves his mother does not hesitate to take a bitter drink or even undergo a painful operation to please her, provided he is huddled in her arms, reassured and encouraged by her.

You too, when the day comes that you really love me, will no longer hesitate to please me by promising some sacrifice and carrying it out faithfully. And when the divine Physician considers it best to apply the cauterizing iron of a trial—sickness, failure, contradiction—you will agree to undergo it to the very end without complaint or struggle, only on condition that you feel yourself cheered by my presence, consoled by my words, fortified by my gentle embrace.

You see, my child, how justified and appropriate is the Church's invocation, "Health of the sick." Make a resolution, therefore, to address it to me for yourself, with your whole heart and at all times, that you may obtain the grace to sustain patiently the infirmities of the body and to be delivered from those of the soul. Do not fail, either, to address it to me often for your brethren, especially when their bodily or spiritual infirmities are brought distressingly to your attention.

REFUGE OF SINNERS

MARY AND THE CONVERSION OF SINNERS

T HE first motive that urges me to work for the conversion of sinners, my child, is *the very love I have for God.*

In the full light of heaven I see the Father continually stretching out His merciful arms toward sinners, inviting them to return to Him. Would I be His most loved and most loving Daughter if I did not labor with all my strength to lead back His prodigal sons, whose conversion gives Him more joy than the perseverance of the faithful children?

I see the Holy Spirit tirelessly knocking, by His predisposing grace, at the door of the sinful soul, that temple which was consecrated to Him by the solemn dedication of Baptism, but from which He has been banished by sin. Would I love this Spirit of love above all things if I did not use every means of persuading the sinner to renounce his sin and receive the divine Guest anew?

Above all, I see Jesus, the Word incarnate, determinedly following the footsteps of His fugitive sheep, entreating him by all His wounds as by so many irresistible voices, to return to Him, his Savior, his Spouse, his All. Would I love Jesus more than myself, would my heart beat in unison with His, would I justly value the blood and tears I saw flowing during His Passion, if I did not burn with a desire to work for the salvation of the poor sinners whom He loves so much and who have cost Him so much?

A second motive that inflames my passion for the conversion of sinners is *the clear vision of the evils* that weigh down their poor souls as long as they remain in their sin.

In the shadowless light of eternity I see how sin defiles the spiritual, immortal soul by plunging it into the mire of carnal, perishable joys; makes it ugly by despoiling it of the wonderful attire of grace and supernatural virtues; darkens it by depriving it of the presence of the divine Guest who was brightening it with His splendor; debases it tremendously by making it, a daughter of God, the servant of the three concupiscences,[1] daughters of the devil; tortures it by giving it only poisoned food or, at most, earthly foods, the best of which are but crumbs, more apt to whet than to appease its appetite for happiness. I see how sin delivers the soul to Satan, who chains it to the side of the abyss and awaits only the end of the trial to drag it with him into eternal torment.

Who indeed could contemplate a distress so poignant with an indifferent heart? The saints (the Curé of Ars, for example) could not think of it without shuddering; and to remedy that distress they did not hesitate to weaken themselves by prayer, work and penance.

But what is the vision of the saints and what is their

---

[1] "All that is in the world is the concupiscence of the flesh, and the concupiscence of the eyes, and the pride of life." *1 John* 2:16.

charity compared to mine? It is the glimmer or warmth of a spark alongside the splendor and heat of the sun.

You may judge from that comparison how eager I feel to sympathize with those unfortunate sinners and to come to their aid. There are such treasures of goodness in my immaculate heart, unobstructed by any selfishness, and the misery of those sinners is shown me in such a light, that I would move heaven and earth to help them even if they were total strangers to me.

But, far from being a stranger, *each one of those unfortunates is for me a son or daughter.*

Yes, every sinner is a child to me—a wounded child, a dead child, but very truly a child, since I as the new Eve was associated with the new Adam in transmitting supernatural life to him.

The sinner is a child loved beyond the power of words to tell, so much that if all the love of other mothers could be put together, it would be only cold ashes alongside the mother love with which I constantly envelop him despite his ingratitude.

Finally, he is a child who has cost me more than I can tell; for, in order to give him birth into the life of grace, I had to feel all the sufferings of Jesus during His Passion exactly as if they were my own. How could I see the offspring of so many tears and sacrifices on the point of being lost, and not fly to his aid?

True, it is through his own fault and his most grievous fault that he has fallen into the devil's trap, having torn himself away from my motherly arms despite my warnings. But a mother easily forgets her child's naughtiness as soon as she sees him in danger or misery. And I am more a Mother than all other mothers together!

It is true also that the mud in which he has wallowed makes him hideous and repulsive. But in such a case does a mother think of anything except to remove the filthy mask of dirt in all haste and find again the beloved features of her little one!

It is true, finally, that even mothers allow themselves to be rebuffed by the more hateful and more obstinate kind of ingratitude. But that cannot happen with me, because God Himself sends me as the ambassador to sinners of His infinite mercy, and to fill this mission He gives me a heart so compassionate that no filth or ugliness can prevent me from pitying the great misery of the sinful soul, a heart so loving that no ingratitude or insult can deter me from tirelessly stretching out my hand to that soul, even to the last minute, to draw it out of the whirlpool.

Having told you why I am so impassioned for the conversion of sinners, I am going to teach you how I help them to be converted.

For conversion *the help of grace is needed before anything else*: if it is easy for man to destroy a life, whether of the body or of the soul, only God can restore it.

But, whereas the sinner has no claim to that grace and is even positively unworthy of it, I have great influence to obtain it for him, both with infinite Mercy by a prayer always heard, and with infinite Justice in exchange for my costly satisfactions of Calvary.

If Jesus could not resist the tears of the widow of Naim, silently imploring the resurrection of her son, how could He resist the tears, incomparably more moving for Him, which He saw me shed at the foot of the cross over the death of every soul that is a victim of sin?

Not content with obtaining the grace of conversion for the sinner who entrusts himself to me, I greatly facilitate his indispensable cooperation with that grace.

To be converted the sinner *must implore pardon,* not so much to persuade God to grant it (thanks to me, that is an accomplished fact!) as to dispose himself to receive it.

Now it may happen that pride dissuades him from admitting his wrongs and asking pardon for them. And when he has enough humility to bow his head and bend his knees, it may happen that shame prevents him from lifting his soiled hands to infinite Holiness and fear prevents him from lifting his criminal hands to infinite Justice.

On the other hand, no matter what mud he has fallen into, he finds no difficulty in addressing me, in whom he sees only a Mother all good and all clement, a Mother before whom he spontaneously assumes the attitude of a little child. And a little child is neither afraid nor ashamed to show his mother his most hideous wounds.

To be converted the sinner *must hope for the pardon* he implores; for no one requests or seeks what he considers impossible.

The devil knows that well. That is why, as soon as he can no longer prevent the desire for pardon, he applies himself to showing the sinner that pardon is impossible, by representing infinite Justice in a light so terrifying and so engrossing that it no longer permits a view of infinite Mercy.

Would not succumbing to that temptation of despair mean

closing to oneself irremediably all access to the grace of salvation?

No! There remains one way for that unfortunate to escape from the dungeon, the vestibule of hell, in which Satan has imprisoned him: to turn his eyes stubbornly to me whom the saints call "the Hope of those who are in despair."[2] For, being Mother of mercy, I am always ready to welcome the miserable, the more tenderly and compassionately as their misery is greater.

Finally, to be converted the sinner *must break with his sinful habits.* Now, because I am Virgin and Immaculate, he cannot live in my presence or even call my image to mind without the sweet rays of my virtue revealing the ugliness of his vices and making him disgusted with them.

On the other hand, because I am a Mother all clement who thinks not of reproaching him for his sins but only of sympathizing with his ills, he does not resist a salutary shame, and he lays himself open little by little to the grace of repentance I have obtained for him.

You see, my child, how I am the Refuge of all sinners, but more particularly of those who pray to me or for whom someone else prays to me. Use every means, therefore, of persuading them to say one prayer to me every day, be it only a Hail Mary. And yourself, borne up by the assurance that you are giving me great pleasure and doing them a great good, do not tire of repeating to me, for them as well as for yourself, "Pray for us sinners."

[2] St. Alphonsus de Liguori, *The Glories of Mary,* part 1, ch. 3, #2, p. 127.

COMFORTER OF THE AFFLICTED

MARY, SUPPORT IN TRIALS

M Y first means of consoling you, my child, is to offer myself to you as an *ideal confidant*.

Confidants here below are not always at your side. As for me, at every hour of day or night I open my heart wide to you, that you may pour into it the overflow of your suffering.

Other confidants have not always the leisure or the patience to listen to you, but I take so much the more pleasure in your confidences when they are more detailed.

Others cannot always understand the nature and extent of your trouble. I recognize instantly what fiber it is of your flesh or your heart that has just been bruised.

Others, finally, do not know how to sympathize effectively with your ordeal even when they understand it, either because they have never experienced it or because they do not love you enough to suffer with you or even to put up with the spectacle of your tears. I, on the other hand, being a symbol of infinite mercy and compassion, being your true Mother and a Mother indescribably tender, am able to be moved sincerely to pity over all your sufferings.

And this is so much the easier for me as I myself have experienced identical or similar sufferings before you. Let me dwell on this last point, of which you are not quite convinced.

Your *body* suffers from cold, hunger, fatigue. Like you I have known the inconveniences and privations of poverty, aggravated during several years by those of exile. Like you I had to earn my bread in the sweat of my brow, bow my shoulders under heavy burdens, bend over a hot fire, harden my hands with the rough tasks of a household; and if I did not experience in my own flesh the pain of blows and wounds, I felt it throughout the Passion in my Son Jesus, to whom an inexpressible love bound me as a nerve to the brain or an artery to the heart.

Your *mind* suffers at its inability to foresee and forestall the dangers hanging over your head.

Was I not the victim of a similar anxiety from the day when the aged Simeon predicted my sword of sorrow without saying when or how I would be stricken?

Your *heart* suffers from the continual affronts of an unsympathetic environment. Did not I, the most Humble and the most Pure, have to live in a world drowned in pride and lust? Did not I, famed Vessel of devotion, have to breathe an air saturated with irreligion and blasphemy? Was not I, Sweetness and Tenderness itself, surrounded by that whirlpool of violence and hate which dragged me, through the sorrowful mysteries, even to Calvary?

I was acquainted likewise with the other wounds of the heart: misunderstanding, when St. Joseph considered putting me out of his house; abandonment, during the three days when the Child Jesus eluded my anxious search; ingratitude, when, reading the future, I saw great numbers of my adopted children pulling away from my motherly arms to surrender to the devil; the most cruel mourning, when death came to take away my relatives, my parents, my spouse, and above all when it came to rob me (after He had been steeped in opprobrium and sorrow before my eyes) of my Son beloved beyond words.

Thus, whatever be the sorrows that trouble you, do not be afraid to come and confide them in me; for, having experienced all of them, I can easily understand and sympathize with them.

But I have a second means, more efficacious still, to console you, and that is to *show you the manifold mercies which the ordeal hides* under its apparent harshness.

In each of the more or less violent blows dealt you by physical or moral suffering I make you see *the jerk on the bridle,* brutal but salutary, by which the divine Driver turns you away from the precipice, or *the lash of the whip* by which He jolts you out of your drowsiness and hurries up your progress in the way of perfection; *the stroke of the pruning hook* by which the Vine-dresser *cuts out* the rotten wood of your evil inclinations and the wild shoots of your purely human tendencies or lovingly *prunes* the healthy branches, the good inclinations, that they may bear more fruit; *the blow on the chisel* by which the divine Sculptor *effaces* in you the last hideous features of the old man, the man of sin, or causes to appear, trait by trait and virtue by virtue, the radiant image of the new man, the adorable resemblance of Jesus.

Finally comes the supreme trial, death. In that hurricane descending on you I will make you feel the *breath* from on high by which the Spirit of God *extinguishes* once and for all the miserable little earthly loves which dispute the heart with supernatural love, or by which He violently *stirs up* that noble supernatural love until it has overrun everything, inflamed everything, divinized everything.

In other words, to the afflicted one who has recourse to me I show clearly that if God's hand makes him feel its harsh touch, that is only to free him from the great evils of sin, the inclination to sin, the punishment due to sin, and to enrich him with the great goods of grace, virtue, merit.

And is it not true that to look at suffering or humiliation from that viewpoint is to make it incomparably sweeter?

Unfortunately, even after having seen clearly the benefits of an ordeal, *you remain inclined to commit numerous faults* which prevent you from making those benefits your own.

Thus, with regard to God, you are inclined to murmur, to distrust, as if He were not equitable or sympathetic enough toward you.

With regard to your brethren, you are inclined unjustly to hold them responsible for your misfortune, to grieve them by your sulky disposition and, more often still, to lack interest in them and think only of your own trouble.

Finally, you have an incorrigible penchant for getting even with the yoke of the cross by seeking illicit compensations: compensations of vanity, eager to publicize its woes in order to make a halo for itself; compensations of sensuality, throwing itself without restraint into the pleasures still permitted.

For the afflicted one who confides in me, I have the power and the mission of procuring the gift of fear which preserves him from these various failings by making him more afraid of offending God than of all other evils, the gift of strength which makes him find the heaviest crosses light by increasing his spiritual energies tenfold, the gift of piety which inclines him to abandon himself with complete trust to his heavenly Father's good pleasure.

See this threefold gift at work in saints like Therese of the Child Jesus or Bernadette. Under the chisel of suffering they are not content to restrain the unruly plunging of nature; they lend themselves and adjust themselves to the divine Sculptor's blows, telling Him, "Do not inconvenience Yourself on my account!"[1] Not content with avoiding what would be a burden to their neighbor, they go on to gladden him by their cheerfulness and smiles. And, far from seeking illicit comforts, they impose on themselves heroic increases of prayer and sacrifice.

But in return they feel their resemblance to Jesus, their capacity for loving God and being loved by Him, their power of intercession and of redemption growing so much that they begin to kiss the hand that strikes them, crying with the Apostle, "I overflow with joy in all my troubles."[2]

Do you want to succeed in carrying the cross in a similar way, my child? Carry it *with me* by considering how I, though innocent, endured much harder trials. Carry it *by me* in asking me continually for the light of grace which alone can reveal the great benefits of suffering, the support of grace

[1] St. Therese, *Novissima Verba*, p. 20.
[2] *2 Cor.* 7:4.

which alone can make you accept it with resignation, if not with love and joy. Finally, carry the cross *for me* by saying, "My Mother, through love for me you accepted the inexpressible agony of Calvary; out of love for you I accept willingly this little insignificant cross which Jesus Himself has just laid on me."

HELP OF CHRISTIANS

MARY AND THE CHURCH

WHY is the Church inexpressibly dear to me, my child? First of all because *it is inexpressibly dear to Jesus.* Jesus loves the Church as His kingdom in which He gathers the redeemed of every tongue and every race into a harmonious unity. He loves it as His spouse through whom He begets into divine life the multitude of souls brought into existence by each new generation. He loves it as His own body which He causes to live, grow and act by an uninterrupted influx of life.

Now my heart is so closely welded to that of Jesus by all the bonds of nature and grace that it is at the same time a need and a joy for me to live in rhythm with Him, to love whatever He loves, in the same way and in the same measure.

How could I help having the same untiring zeal, then, to defend that kingdom against the schemes of the prince of darkness and his accomplices, the same solicitude to take care of that mystical body exposed to so many dangers?

Besides being Christ's kingdom, *the Church is also my own kingdom*, first by right of donation: as evidence of His filial love and deference, Jesus saw fit to associate me with His universal reign over spiritual and temporal societies; then by right of conquest: I cooperated with Jesus and through Jesus to conquer it over Satan at the price of the sufferings of my whole life and my unspeakable agony on Calvary. And these two titles make the Church equally dear to me.

Again, the Church is very dear to me because *it cooperates with me,* at every moment and at every point on the globe, in the work nearest my heart: the dispensing of grace, the bearing of souls into divine life.

This role has earned for the Church the name of spouse of Christ. But she fills the role only with me and through me. I am the heart receiving the life-giving grace directly from Jesus; she is the network of arteries striving ever more to envelop and compenetrate the human mass, in order to place that precious life within reach of every soul.

Finally, I feel compelled to love the Church as a mother feels compelled to love *the child born of her.*

The Church was born of the merits Christ heaped up during His life and especially at the hour of His death. I was associated with Christ to merit in equity all that He was meriting in justice for the human race.[1]

Thus, just as I conceived, carried and gave birth to Christ by my virginal flesh, so by my merit I conceived, carried and gave birth to the Church which is His mystical body.

What wonder, then, that the Holy Spirit inspired in me a truly maternal tenderness and solicitude for the Church?

How can I help the Church? First of all by my function as Mediatrix which confers on me the power and the mission

---

[1] Pius **X**, *Ad diem illum.*

of obtaining for it all the graces necessary for its preservation or its growth.

In fact, after the Ascension *I obtain for it* without delay *the coming of that live-giving Spirit* without whom it is nothing but a motionless germ, incapable of evolving and gathering men to itself.[2]

After Pentecost *I obtain for it those exceptional graces* which alone, by making miracles spring up in its footsteps, have enabled it to maintain and propagate itself in a world of enemies.

During the three centuries of violent persecution I obtain for its weakest members—old men, young girls, children—*the gift of fortitude* which permits them to stand the worst tortures with serenity as well as endurance; for example, my daughter Blandina, tortured from dawn to nightfall without anyone's being able to extort any confession from her but this: "I am a Christian woman."[3]

Unable to destroy the Church by violence, paganism seeks to corrupt it by a civilization saturated with vice. I preserve it against this new danger no less grave by raising up everywhere hosts of virgins who by the example of their heroic chastity cause a current of pure air to circulate in that polluted atmosphere.

This twofold danger reappears often in the course of the centuries, but I never fail to intervene as soon as it threatens to become fatal to the Church.

Thus, when pagan nations are on the point of submerging

---

[2] Pius XII, *On the Mystical Body*, #110.
[3] Eusebius Pamphili, *Ecclesiastical History*, translated by Roy J. Deferrari (New York: Fathers of the Church, Inc., 1953), book 5, ch. 1, p. 277.

the Church, I obtain a victory as brilliant as it is unexpected; for example, the victory of Las Navas de Tolosa in which Catholic Spain fighting under my banner stops the invasion of the Moors;[4] or the victories no less decisive at Lepanto and at Vienna, commemorated by the feasts of the Rosary and of the Holy Name of Mary!

Do perils from within follow upon those from without? Does *the luxuriant vegetation of the concupiscences* threaten to smother the fine supernatural graft on the tree of the Church? I come to the aid of the Church in two ways. On the one hand I inspire the hierarchy to promote such reforms as will curb undisciplined conduct. On the other hand I obtain from infinite Mercy the birth in the Church of great saints, powerful in word and deed: vigorous shoots which, by drawing in immense reserves of sap, soon regenerate the enfeebled graft and enrich it with abundant foliage, capable of replacing the dried up branches or even the great limbs hacked off by schism and heresy.

Is not that what my sons and daughters have done by themselves or by their religious families: Benedict and Bernard, Francis and Dominic, Ignatius of Loyola and Teresa of Avila, and their numerous emulators?

Does it come about that the mystical vine is *attacked even in its root which is the faith?* To those who deny the true faith I oppose great Doctors: to Arius, St. Athanasius; to Nestorius, St. Cyril; to Pelagius, St. Augustine; to Luther and Calvin, St. Peter Canisius, St. Robert Bellarmine and St. Francis de Sales.

After refuting the heresiarchs by the Doctors I have them

[4] Georges Goyau, *Histoire Religieuse de la France,* p. 236.

condemned by the Councils. And all this is so truly my work that the liturgy does not hesitate to proclaim that it is I alone who have "trampled down all heresies in the whole world."[5]

If the faith is compromised not by a false doctrine but by a terrible scandal such as the great schism when it is no longer known who is the true head of the Church, I come to strengthen it by letting Christendom see saints of a holiness so vivid as to capture everyone's attention: St. Catherine of Siena, advisor to Popes; St. Colette, famous ecstatic; St. Vincent Ferrer, sowing miracles by the thousand. And in that long night their passage is like a luminous trail which forestalls any doubt about the light.

In these days when everything conspires to kill the faith of the Church both by starvation and by suffocation, I come myself to give it life by multiplying apparitions and miracles (think of Lourdes and Fatima!) whose first result is to put every man of good will in contact with the supernatural.

Finally, at all times I restrain by my queenly power the fury of Satan, who strives unremittingly to ally against the Church all her enemies within and without, to fan the flame of their hatred and unify their attacks.

Now that you know my power and my desire to help the holy Church, my child, do not fail to commend all her needs to me.

You take pleasure in dreaming of terrible reprisals against the modern persecutors who discredit her by their calumnies, hamper or despoil her by irreligious legislation and threaten her even with the worst violence.

[5] Common of feasts of the Blessed Virgin Mary, 3rd nocturn, 7th antiphon.

Those dreams may foster your self love, but they render no service to the Church. On the other hand, you will render her a great service if you apply yourself by earnest, continual prayer to calling down my all-powerful protection on her; for the law imposed on each member, "Ask and you shall receive," applies also to the mystical body. And since the body can call me to its aid only through the voices of its members, the more numerous those voices are, the more easily can I come to its aid.

QUEEN OF ANGELS

MARY'S REIGN OVER THE ANGELS

"THE holy Mother of God has been exalted above the choirs of angels, to the heavenly kingdom."[1] "Hail, Queen of the heavens, hail, Mistress of angels!"[2]

For centuries, my child, the liturgy has proclaimed in these words that I am truly the Queen of the angels. *For what reasons did God choose to associate me* in Christ's reign over the angels?

He willed it *by reason of wisdom.* It is a requirement of order that in a perfect city like the heavenly one the lower be ruled by the higher; and am I not incomparably higher than the angels in dignity, in function, in perfection! It is a requirement of order that in a perfect family like the heavenly one the King's Mother have power and dominion over all His servants; and have not all the heavenly spirits been designated servants of the Word incarnate?

He willed it *by reason of fidelity* to this solemn promise: "Everyone who exalts himself shall be humbled, and he who

---

[1] 2nd Vespers of the Assumption, verse.
[2] Antiphon *Ave Regina caelorum.*

humbles himself shall be exalted!"[3] Recognizing that whatever was estimable or praiseworthy in myself came from
God, I referred every bit of esteem or praise to Him. Recognizing that I was all God's and for God, I had the constant
disposition of putting my whole being and all my possessions
at the service of God, and even at the service of the least of
His creatures: "Behold the handmaid of the Lord."[4] That is
why God, while punishing Lucifer's pride and rebellion by
hurling him into the depths of hell, exalts me above all
creatures to reward the humility that led me to place myself
below all and at the service of all.

God willed to associate me in Christ's reign over the angels
to satisfy His justice, which binds itself not to leave unre-
warded the least sacrifice accepted for His glory. Jesus accepts
the humiliations of the Passion in order to serve His Father's
redemptive plan. In return His Father grants Him by right
of merit that universal kingdom to which He was already
entitled by right of inheritance.[5] To serve the same redemptive plan I agree to share all the humiliations of Jesus. In
return God associates me in the reign of Jesus over angels as
well as men.

Above all, He willed it *to satisfy His love.* Because the
three divine Persons love me more than all other creatures,
it is a need and a joy to Them to give me power and authority
over all, including the most exalted. And with regard to the
Word incarnate especially, it is a need and a joy to Him to
show me His indescribable love, His unique love, by associating me in those privileges and excellences which He shares

[3] *Luke* 14:11.
[4] *Luke* 1:38.
[5] *Phil.* 2:8-11; *Eph.* 1:19-21.

with no other: being Redeemer and Mediator, He wants me
to be Co-Redeemer and Co-Mediator; being King of angels
and men and all creation, He wants me to share that royalty
with Him.

For their part, the angels acquiesce with their whole mind
and their whole heart in the divine decree which constitutes
me their Queen.

The fact is that in their thirst for truth and justice they
are always ready to recognize the superiority and authority
of anyone put over them by the sovereign Master.

And *in me they perceive a threefold transcendence.*

First they see *a transcendence of election* or predestination.
While they have been predestined to be the first servants of
the Word incarnate, with the mission of carrying out His
orders, adoring His greatness and singing His praises, they see
me chosen among all creatures to be His true Mother, with the
mission of giving Him the attentions, caresses and counsels
that a little child expects from his mother, and the right to
receive from Him the deference, gratitude and filial love that
a child owes to the author of its being.

In the second place they perceive and revere in me *a transcendence of beauty and perfection.*

Each of their nine choirs reflects more particularly one
divine perfection: the Seraphim, love; the Cherubim, light;
the Dominations, grandeur; the Virtues, power ... By myself
I reflect all those same perfections, and with incomparably
greater brilliance, so great that it seems to demand even
God's admiration: "How beautiful you are, my Love, how
beautiful!"[6]

[6] *Cant.* 4:1.

Those nine choirs united send up unceasingly to God an indescribable symphony. My praise by itself constitutes a more perfect symphony; for my mind ranges farther over the ocean of the divine perfections than even the vision of the Cherubim, and my heart breathes out to that infinite Beauty a flame of love incomparably more ardent than that of the Seraphim.

That is why those heavenly spirits are happy to contemplate in me as in a faithful mirror the more dazzling rays of divine beauty and glory which they cannot contemplate face to face. And in order to give their canticle of praise an increase of perfection they are happy to unite it to the Canticle of canticles which is my "Magnificat."

Finally, they perceive and revere in me *a transcendence of function.* Whereas they themselves have only a mission of guardians and guides to the elect, they see that I am the true Mother of the elect; a Mother who, after meriting for them the life of grace, dispenses it to them throughout their trial with a real mother's tenderness and care. Moreover, the heavenly spirits exercise that very function of guardian of souls as my agents and servants, as bearers of one of those graces of which I am constituted universal Dispenser.

Enraptured by the unceasing vision of that threefold transcendence, the nine choirs of angels keep blessing God for having appointed me their Queen, and repeating to me the *canticle of gratitude and love, admiration and veneration,* by which on the day of my Assumption they celebrated my enthronement at Christ's right hand:

"To you the homage of *our gratitude!* By cooperating in the redemptive work at the price of your martyrdom on Calvary, you have filled the voids left in our ranks by the defection of the rebellious angels.

"To you the homage of *our love!* We love whatever God loves, and God loves you more than all other creatures together.

"To you the homage of *our admiration!* Are you not the masterpiece in which the Creator is pleased to gather all the rays of grace or beauty scattered over all other beings? Are you not the ornament and the glory of our kingdom?

"And how could we refuse you the homage of *our obedience,* when we see our King make it His joy to fulfill your least desires? the homage of *our veneration,* when we see our God showing you so much consideration and honor?"

What sentiments should be inspired in you, my child, by the thought of my glorious reign over all the heavenly spirits?

Toward Jesus: a lively feeling of gratitude for His having seen fit to repay by such exaltation and glory the abasements and humiliations I accepted out of love for you during the Passion.

Toward me: an increase of gratitude and love, that she who enjoys the love and the praise of angels whenever she will, condescends to be pleased with your childish babbling, your flickering candle and your quickly faded flowers; but also an increase of respect and veneration, for a miserable worm should not dare permit himself all manner of familiarity with her whom the princes of heaven surround with all manner of respect!

Finally, *with regard to the angels* themselves the thought of my glorious reign over them should inspire you to ask them often for a large share of their love and gratitude toward me, and likewise to give them often the mandate of praising, thanking and loving me in your stead, in order to make up for the insufficiency or the unworthiness of your own homage. You may be sure that such a mandate will be accepted with joy!

QUEEN OF PATRIARCHS

MARY, TEACHER OF OUR HOPE

T HE Holy Spirit offers you the patriarchs, my child, as models of hope: "Strangers and pilgrims on the earth . . . they longed after a better, that is, a heavenly country."[1]

In your heart *the desire for heaven* appears only as a rare, passing glimmer. All aflame for perishable joys, you have only forgetfulness and indifference for the place of eternal glory and beatitude Jesus has prepared for you in paradise.

And yet he who does not ardently desire the end is very little concerned with the means. The happiness of heaven is a gift promised for prayer and at the same time a reward assigned for merit.[2] But how will you be zealous to implore that gift with tears and earn that reward in the sweat of your brow if you do not desire it, if you hardly ever think of it?

Know, then, that I have the mission and the power of *giving birth* to the desire for heaven in your heart: "I am the Mother of holy hope."[3]

---

[1] *Heb.* 11:13-16.

[2] Council of Trent, Decree on Justification, ch. 16; Denzinger-Bann-wart-Umberg, *Enchiridion Symbolorum,* #809, pp. 293-294.

[3] *Ecclus.* 24:24; Epistle of the Motherhood of the Blessed Virgin Mary.

Yes, I teach everyone who has a great devotion for me to desire heaven with an *unceasing desire,* like that of the exile on the way to the father's house, never distracted from the end pursued by the concerns or the pleasures of the journey; with an *ardent desire,* like that of the thirsty hind rushing to the spring of living water;[4] like that of the runner pressing on with outstretched hands toward the goal where fortune and glory await him;[5] with an *overruling desire,* which makes the happiness of paradise the principal object of his thoughts and concerns, joys and sorrows, hopes and fears, efforts and sacrifices: "I count all things as dung, that I may gain Christ";[6] finally, with a *trusting desire,* which does not let itself be troubled by any apprehension. If this good servant begins to fear the numerous enemies that bar his way, I answer him with the Apostle, "If God is for us, who is against us?"[7] If he begins to fear his own weakness: "He who did not spare even His own Son, but delivered Him up for us all—how will He not also freely give us all things along with Him,"[8] all the helps necessary or useful? If he begins to fear on account of his many sins: "Where sin abounded, grace super-abounded."[9] Moreover, how could he cast any doubt on the tenderness and mercy of his heavenly Father when he sees Him make use of my motherly hands to guide and defend him, my motherly heart to condescend to his littleness, put up with his defects, pardon his faults?

After having kindled in your soul this constant, ardent, trusting desire for heaven, I have the mission and the power of *maintaining and intensifying it* more and more by teach-

4 *Psalm* 41:2.   7 *Rom.* 8:31.
5 *Phil.* 3:13-14.   8 *Rom.* 8:32.
6 *Phil.* 3:8.   9 *Rom.* 5:20.

ing you to *substitute* the desire of eternal joys immediately for any desire of perishable joys that may begin to appear in your heart.

For example, does it occur to you to envy the *riches* that people around you are seeking with feverish activity? Through my grace and example I lead you to say, "I have to obtain a better treasure and a better inheritance: a treasure of merits which in heaven will be changed into a treasure of glory and beatitude; a heritage of divine, eternal life which I shall share with Christ."

Are you tempted to overestimate, perhaps at the expense of your sanctification, the *knowledge* of this world, corroded by forgetfulness and annihilated by death? I make you think of the knowledge of heaven, which fathoms everything knowable without fatigue or error because it is enlightened not by the pale reflections of creation but by the very source of uncreated Light.

Do you feel frustrated at being unable to satisfy your eyes with some displays of *beauty* too dangerous or too far away? I make you say, "What are the splendors of this universe compared to the ones that will be shown me in the new heavens and the new earth! What are the festivals and spectacles of our earthly cities compared to those of the heavenly Jerusalem! What is the charm of a human face alongside the beauty of the saints and angels, the beauty of the Virgin, the beauty of Jesus, above all the infinite beauty of the three divine Persons, the contemplation of which will plunge me into a constantly renewed ecstasy!"

Does your heart make you feel too keenly its *thirst to love and be loved?* I remind you of the various forms of love reserved for you in paradise: love from each of the angels, from each of the elect, even those most distant from you in origin or culture; love from the heavenly Mother, who will then reveal herself in her inexpressible sweetness; love even more ineffable from the holy soul of Jesus, who will associate you with His happiness, His glory and His power; absolutely incomprehensible love from the three divine Persons, whose embrace will beatify your soul by fulfilling its deepest aspiration, to adhere without partition to the sovereign Good: "Let Him kiss me with the kiss of His mouth!"[10]

Are you attracted, *fascinated by a joy* that passes within your reach? If it is bad or dangerous, I make you say, "Away with that cumbersome, begriming refuse! I want a joy worthy of the nobility of my soul, daughter of God and spouse of Christ." If it is lawful but imperfect, I make you say, "Away with those poor crumbs fallen under God's table, for I aspire to sit at the table itself, to taste the joys which alone can satisfy my soul's hunger! Away with those deceptive reflections which fade and vanish in the twinkling of an eye! The joy for which I reserve all my desires is steeped in a Light that does not decline, a Beauty that does not fade, a love that does not grow cold!"

Do you catch yourself wishing for *the esteem of men,* an honorable place, some bit of superiority or authority? I tell you, "Aspire after a better authorized praise, that which Christ decrees in the presence of God and His angels: 'He who overcomes ... I will acknowledge his name before My Father and before His angels.'[11] Aspire after a more glorious

---

[10] *Cant.* 1:1.
[11] *Apoc.* 3:5.

place, one which will seat you beside the immortal King of ages: 'He who overcomes, I will permit him to sit with Me upon My throne.'[12] Aspire to a higher dominion, one which will associate you with Christ's lordship and magistracy: 'To him who overcomes ... I will give authority over the nations.' "[13]

Finally, when you groan under the weight of a crushing or exacting *labor,* I invite you to desire the eternal, beatifying rest that awaits you in the fatherland. When you are anguished to see yourself always exposed to violent *temptations* and dangerous traps, I make you desire a state of absolute security under the very wings of the Almighty. When you are under the pressure of a *trial,* I make you sigh after the blessed abode that excludes tears and moans, sorrow, contradiction and mourning.

That is how I can make you realize easily, my child, the Apostle's program, "Seek the things that are above ... set your mind on the things that are above";[14] a program that can reorient your heart always toward eternal joys, despite the incessant oscillations given it by the fear of a sacrifice or the attractions of a transitory pleasure.

That you may obtain in abundance, however, that precious grace of the desire for heaven, you must pray much to me. And that you may correspond readily to it, you must love me much. For nothing is easier than to lift up your heart to me, so meek, so compassionate, so appealing; and to lift it up to me is to lift it up to heaven!

---

[12] *Apoc.* 3:21.
[13] *Apoc.* 2:26.
[14] *Col.* 3:12.

QUEEN OF PROPHETS

MARY AND THE MILITANTS

T HE prophet's first function was to *announce the future*. I am the Queen of prophets because my virginal motherhood was the object of their predictions and because I myself made a prediction about my destiny which has never lacked fulfillment through twenty centuries: "All generations shall call me blessed!"[1]

Strange as this prophecy was on the lips of a lowly Galilean woman who had only to go out of her village to be unknown by all, it has been realized to the letter.

To be convinced of this, my child, you need only try to count how many shrines, statues, pictures, masterpieces of every kind have been dedicated to me in all ages and all countries; how many religious have consecrated themselves to my service; how many saints or pious souls have shown me an ardent devotion; how many tokens of praise and love have risen up to me from men in every quarter of the earth, from angels and

[1] *Luke* 1:48.

saints in every quarter of heaven! Yes, all generations shall call me blessed in time and in eternity.

But the prophets had not only the mission of foretelling the future. Above all they were *witnesses to God*: witnesses to His favors and His rights, His promises and His threats. Thus John the Baptist, who never made any prediction, is called "a prophet and more than a prophet,"[2] because he excelled in this role of witness to the Word incarnate.

Under the new Law every baptized person and more particularly everyone who is confirmed receives the mission and the grace of bearing witness to Christ by word and example before all those who do not know Him, who forget or deny Him.

Now it is I who *have merited for you,* through and with Jesus, this mission of witness to Christ; and it is I who *dispense the grace for it to you,* as I merited and dispensed it to John the Baptist.

First I can obtain for you (on condition that you ask me) all the graces necessary to be *a witness to Christ by your words.*

To inspire in you a lively desire to make Jesus and His message known around you, I keep reminding you that this is a way of showing the Savior a deep gratitude and a great love, by revealing Him to those who do not know Him: "In the midst of you is standing One whom you do not know!";[3] a way of rendering your brethren a priceless service, for "there is no salvation in any other";[4] a way of assuring yourself a splendid reward, for Jesus will pay a hundredfold for the services you have rendered His members and the glory you have procured for Himself.

[2] *Luke* 7:26.
[3] *John* 1:26.
[4] *Acts* 4:12.

Conversely, I keep reminding you that to neglect through laziness or faintheartedness to spread Christ's message around you is to incur the sovereign Master's reproach: "As for the unprofitable servant, cast him forth into the darkness outside,"[5] because he has not made that most precious talent of all, the "knowledge of salvation,"[6] bear fruit; it is to incur the reproach of souls: "We were hungry for God's word, and you did not think to give us even a few crumbs of the bread of Christian truth which you possessed in abundance"; it is to incur the reproaches of your own conscience: would you not be ashamed to see the irreligious more zealous in sowing tares than you are in sowing the good seed, more zealous in denying Christ than you are in affirming Him, more zealous in impeding His reign than you are in preparing a way for it in minds and hearts!

Besides being a witness to Christ by your speech you must be one even more *by your example*. Through your exemplary Christian life you should act on your environment like a light which imperceptibly but very effectively brings health and fertility.

The most irreligious who refuse to listen to your word are most inclined, at the same time, to examine your conduct as a Christian and a militant. If your conduct reproduces the Savior's, it reveals to them unwittingly the ideal of purity, religion and charity which He came to bring to the world.

Ordinary souls are too frivolous to meditate on Christ's message or let anyone explain it to them. If you live it integrally, your example reveals it to them clearly and without

[5] *Matt.* 25:30.
[6] *Luke* 1:77.

effort. They are too fainthearted to commit themselves to the rugged paths of the Christian life. Not content with proving that life practicable, your example draws them into its paths by an irresistible attraction.

That this result may be achieved, however, your good example must be total; for a single vice can destroy the effect of ten virtues. It must have a certain brilliance; for virtue does not attract attention and become contagious except in so far as it rises above the common level.

Now it is only too evident that, left to your own resources, you are absolutely incapable of giving your neighbors such example for long. You even risk being blinded yourself by the mirages of your environment instead of enlightening it with the light of Christ, and letting yourself be contaminated by its corruption instead of healing it.

On the other hand, if you assure yourself of my exceptional aid by an exceptional devotion, I will obtain for you the strength in every encounter to bear Jesus the twofold witness of word and example, despite the combined efforts of the flesh, the world and the devil to suppress that witness.

In the same degree in which you must be zealous to prepare the way for the reign of Jesus by your word and example, you must be concerned with preparing the way for your own witness by *prayer and sacrifice.*

Before coming "to bear witness to the Light"[7] the Precursor lived a long time in prayer and propitiation. The fact is that only the Holy Spirit can effect the passage from incredulity to faith, from the state of sin to that of grace, from lukewarmness to fervor. But ordinarily He does not descend into

[7] *John* 1:8.

a soul to effect this work of life except in so far as He is
called: "Ask and you shall receive."[8]

Since the unbeliever and the sinner are hardly concerned
with imploring the Holy Spirit, it is you who must do so in
their stead. Otherwise, no matter how profusely you sow the
good seed of your word or example in those souls, it will
fall on dry rock where it cannot take root.

Actually you risk praying very little and very poorly for
souls, for want of seeing their terrible distress and for want of
having a tender compassion on them. You risk also not being
heard, because you have little influence with God.

If you cultivate devotion to me, I will obtain for you a
living faith to prevent you from losing sight of the excruci-
ating misery of souls, a tender compassion which will urge
you to pray unceasingly for them, not in a perfunctory way
but with that fervor of desire and that perseverance to which
you are accustomed when you implore the most ardently desired favors for yourself.

Moreover, the more you increase in love of me, the more
compassionate will your heart become in imitation of mine,
and the more also will it increase in love of those who are
my true children.

I will obtain for you likewise a great influence with God
on behalf of souls.

Your influence is measured by the degree to which God
is pleased in you, consequently by the degree of your humility,
purity, charity. And I have shown you elsewhere that you
quickly become humble, pure and loving when you live close
to me.

[8] *Luke* 11:9.

Moreover, God loves me so much that He cannot fail to be pleased with those who love me and to receive their prayer favorably. And if their prayer is really too unworthy to obtain the precious graces they are asking for their brethren, He readily consents to have me join my own prayer to it, which has all power both to sway infinite Mercy and to disarm infinite Justice.

You see, my child, how devotion to me will facilitate your threefold task of witness to Christ before men: making Christ's law known to them by your words, proving by your example that it is possible and desirable to submit to that law, obtaining for them by your prayer the grace to accept and fufill all its requirements.

QUEEN OF APOSTLES

MARY AND THE PRIEST

IN the first place, my child, every apostle invested with the priesthood must *continue the mission I had with regard to the Word incarnate.*

However desirable might have been *the coming and the presence* of the incarnate Word in this world, God did not choose to bring it about without my consent and cooperation. Just so, however desirable may be the coming and the presence of Jesus-Host in the churches of your cities or villages, it will never occur without the priest's consent and cooperation.

The Infant Jesus gave Himself over entirely to me, that *I might take care of His sacred body,* procure a dwelling place for Him, rescue Him from His persecutors and present Him to His friends, the shepherds, the magi, the aged Simeon.

The Host Jesus, having reduced Himself to a still greater helplessness, abandons Himself in the same way to the solicitude of His priest. It is to the priest that He entrusts the sweet and noble charge of taking care of His Eucharistic body, procuring a suitable dwelling for Him, preserving Him from outrage by men and damage by the elements, giving Him in Communion to His friends and refusing Him to the unworthy and sacrilegious.

Not understood by this world of darkness, Jesus chose to make me *His intimate confidant.*

In the same way He lavishes graces of light on His priest to impart a deeper knowledge of His message and His Person: "To you it is given to know the mysteries of the kingdom of God."[1]

Finally, on Calvary Jesus did not choose to consummate *His sacrifice* without asking my consent and participation. On the altar, Jesus does not choose to renew His sacrifice unless His lowly minister is willing to consent to it and cooperate in it; and He invites the priest likewise to be associated with Him as victim.

In the second place, the priest is *associated in my mission with regard to souls.*

I have told you elsewhere how, having merited supernatural life for all men in general, I keep working from on high to give birth to that precious life in each one of them, nourish that budding life, protect, heal and resuscitate that fragile life until it is changed into a life of glory.

Following my example, the priest cooperates to give birth to supernatural life in souls by administering Baptism to them. He nourishes it and makes it grow by procuring for them the bread of grace through his prayers, the bread of truth through his preaching, the Eucharistic Bread through Communion. He heals supernatural life and, if need be, resuscitates

[1] *Luke* 8:10.

it by applying the blood of Christ to souls through absolution. He prepares it to unfold into the life of glory by procuring the last sacraments for them.

But it is not only *in imitation of me* that he exercises this spiritual motherhood with regard to souls; it is *in dependence on me,* as my instrument and my helper.

See what takes place, for example, in the conversion of a sinner. The grace of conversion must be implored. As the sinner neglects or refuses to pray, I inspire the priest to pray in his stead; sometimes I even incline him to join propitiation to supplication, in order to override the veto of infinite Justice for a too protracted abuse of grace: think of the penances of the Curé of Ars!

The grace of conversion must be welcomed with all its requirements: remorse, confession, reparation. I inspire the priest with the exhortations or approaches most apt to bring about acceptance of these requirements.

Finally, absolution must come to make the contrition fruitful. I obtain the grace that the absolution be given validly by the priest and received fruitfully by the sinner.

In a word, the priest needs grace that he may be willing and able to instruct, convert and sanctify the faithful; the faithful need grace that they may be willing and able to let themselves be instructed, converted and sanctified. And am I not the Dispenser of all graces without exception?

In the third place, I have the power and the mission of *obtaining for the priest all the virtues* necessary to fulfill his priestly functions well with respect to Jesus or with respect to souls.

Jesus is the hidden God. To serve Him well requires *a lively faith.* Constantly enlightened by an intense spirit of faith, I knew how to perceive and revere infinite Majesty at every moment in the tiny newborn whom I pressed to my heart; infinite Fulness in the little pauper whom I had to warm, feed and clothe; infinite Power in the helpless infant whom I had to carry in my arms.

For the priest diligent in meditating my example and imploring my intercession, I obtain a like spirit of faith which permits him never to lose sight of the God-Man hidden under the veil of the Eucharistic species, and which inclines him to treat the sacred Host with supreme reverence.

Jesus is the thrice holy God. To serve Him well requires *great purity of heart and body.*

My intellect, my memory, my imagination were so possessed by the Savior's human and divine beauty that they showed themselves impervious to all earthly attractions. And my heart was so inflamed with love of Him that earthly affections could not touch upon it without being either annihilated or transmuted instantly into that love. What pleasure the Lamb who feeds in the midst of the lilies must have taken in my company, my services, my caresses!

Let the priest become used to living in the irradiation of my purity, and his lips, which he must lend to Jesus for consecration and absolution, will soon be purified of all trivial, uncharitable, vain speech; his eyes, which contemplate Christ's thrice holy body so closely, will quickly free themselves of all frivolous curiosity; his memory, his imagination, his intellect, which must become irradiated with Christ's truth, will no longer be clouded or soiled with those troubled images which sometimes arise from their shallows like an unhealthy fog; his heart will be forever freed from those miserable little loves which prevent him from being totally possessed by the great and noble love of Jesus.

Jesus is Love itself. To serve Him worthily requires *a very high degree of charity.* In me the priest finds the example and the grace of a perfect love for Jesus: an impassioned love that will keep his soul gravitating around the tabernacle; an active love that finds its happiness in taking up all sorts of labors and cares for Jesus; a valiant love that does not expect the Savior to leave His cross at the door when He comes to visit us.

In me the priest finds also the example and the grace of a perfect love for souls, members of Jesus.

First of all I give him a share in my *motherly compassion* by opening his ear and his heart to the appeal of souls starved for the truth of the Gospel and the Bread of the Eucharist, which he alone can dispense to them; to the appeal of souls terribly defiled by sin and sighing after the purification of Christ's blood which he alone can apply to them; to the appeal of souls chained by Satan on the edge of the abyss and imploring a deliverance which he alone can procure for them.

At the same time I give him a share in my *motherly devotion* which has induced me to spare nothing, even my own Son, to procure the salvation of souls. Let the priest apply himself to cultivating devotion to me more every day, and he will soon make his own the Apostle's heroic program: "I will most gladly spend and be spent myself for your souls, even though, loving you more, I be loved less."[2]

[2] *2 Cor.* 12:15.

As to the faithful, convinced that I am the Dispenser of the innumerable graces required to make a good priest, they will keep asking God for those graces through my intercession. Thus, despite their lack of much influence, they will respond effectively to the Savior's desire, "Pray the Master of the harvest to send out laborers into His harvest."[3] And they will have a share in the good accomplished by those good priests: "He who receives" (who assists) "a prophet because he is a prophet shall receive a prophet's reward."[4]

[3] *Luke* 10:2.
[4] *Matt.* 10:41.

QUEEN OF MARTYRS

PRICE OF MARY'S CO-REDEMPTION

A S my martyrdom was exclusively *a martyrdom of the heart,* the only way to get an idea of it, my child, is to consider the terrible contradiction inflicted on my love by the drama of Calvary.

God alone can measure my love for Jesus. At the Annunciation He Himself confers on me a mother love worthy of an Infant-God, consequently inexpressible and inconceivable. And this power of loving encounters in my virginal heart no attachment that can hinder it, nor does it encounter in Jesus any defect that might cool its ardor. And for thirty-three years grace unites with nature to keep intensifying that incomparable mother love more and more: incessant outpourings of the Holy Spirit; continual community of life, prayers, sacrifices; uninterrupted exchange of services, confidences, tokens of affection and gratitude.

Then during the Passion, with the eyes of the body or those of the soul I have to contemplate, one by one, all the exterior and interior sufferings of that dear Son, so lovable and so loved.

For hours *I must contemplate sin,* the pitiless executioner, *intent upon the virginal flesh of Jesus.*[1] It is not enough to have bruised that flesh by binding Him and striking Him. Sin thirsts for His blood; and so it ties Him to the pillar and has His flesh torn to shreds under the lash of the scourges. Having spared His head in this first torture, sin encircles it with a crown of thorns which it pounds in with a stick. Then throughout the sorrowful journey sin grinds His flesh under the weight of the cross, to force still more sweat and blood from it. Finally when Jesus, exhausted, reaches the summit of Calvary, sin gives Him for a bed the wood of the gibbet to which it fastens Him with four nails.

My eyes wide with fright and horror, I must contemplate every one of those cruelties. And, united to Jesus and identified with Him as I am, I cannot see them without feeling most keenly in my heart all that He endures in His flesh. Yes, my heart is truly bruised by each blow of the scourge that draws blood from His back, torn by each of the thorns pressed down into His brow, crushed by the cross that burdens His shoulders, transfixed by the nails that pierce His hands and feet.

Not content to crucify the body of Jesus, *sin tortures His soul by loading it with disgrace.* I am not to miss any of this second spectacle either, no less distressing for my heart.

All night this cruel executioner has left my dear Son to the scoffing of servants. Now it drags Him in broad daylight from one tribunal to another, like the worst of criminals.

[1] Feast of the Sacred Heart, hymn of Vespers: "For this it was pierced by a lance ... that it might cleanse us from our sins."

Before Herod it delivers Him to the scornful mockery of the nobility; before Pilate, to the buffoonery of the soldiers who cover Him with blows and spittle, then to the derision of all the people: "Behold the Man!"[2] "Not this Man, but Barabbas!"[3] To put an end to Him it hangs Him between two criminals on a gibbet at the foot of which His triumphant enemies taunt Him with their defiance and their sarcasm: "If You are the Son of God, come down from the cross!"[4]

And I too stay at the foot of the cross to receive all those successive waves of shame and disgrace which descend on my heart like a flood after passing over the soul of Jesus!

At the same time that it is loading the soul of Jesus with opprobrium, *sin plunges His soul into an ocean of bitterness.* And I must contemplate and share this third torture.

Benefactor, Friend, Spouse, Savior of all souls, Jesus sees from the height of His cross how the crowds surrounding Him, and behind them the many generations of all ages and all countries, receive His supreme act of devotion, by which He rescues them from sin and hell and merits eternal life for them.

Alas! He has the sorrow of seeing His love, so noble and compassionate, strong and tender, persistent and gentle, being bruised against three stone walls. First the insatiable hatred of His enemies: scribes or Pharisees, sectarians of all the centuries furiously bent on slandering Him, proscribing Him, stirring up the multitude against Him: "We do not wish this Man to be king over us!"[5] Again, His love is bruised

2 *John* 19:5.
3 *John* 18:40.
4 *Matt.* 27:40.
5 *Luke* 19:14.

against the wall of the indifference of the masses, completely absorbed in their earthly concerns, who do not take the time to consider how much He loved us, how much He suffered for us. Finally, it meets the wall of the ingratitude of His most beloved friends, the ones most overwhelmed with favors: the treason of Judas who betrays Him to satisfy greed; the cowardice of Peter who denies Him out of fear or human respect; the faintheartedness of the disciples who are quite willing to follow Him as long as it costs them nothing, but take flight as soon as they see even the shadow of the cross appearing! How this rends His tender, loving heart! And how it rends mine, beating ever in unison with His by nature and by grace!

Yet Jesus suffers more from *the outrage committed by sin against His Father* than from the outrage done to His own love. His marvelous infused knowledge (by which He knows everything) lets Him see with pitiless clarity all the sins that have been committed or will be committed: a black army covering the whole surface of the earth, the whole course of the ages, and ceaselessly vomiting floods of filth and hatred! The One against whom these outrages mount up is His heavenly Father, infinitely adorable and infinitely loved. And the ones who offer these insults are His own brethren, His own members!

Having received some light on the malice of sin, St. Grignion de Montfort cries, "Would it not be better for me to die than to see You, my God, so cruelly offended every day? . . . A thousand deaths would be more bearable to me!"[6] What sorrow, then, must be felt by the incomparably more clear-sighted and more loving soul of Jesus!

[6] *Vraie Dévotion,* appendix, p. 52.

Those, my child, are some inklings of the martyrdom of Jesus. And *my martyrdom is not other than His.*

Francis of Assisi contemplates with a great love the wounds of Jesus crucified, and that love like a sword imprints the sacred stigmata on his hands and feet.

My love, greater than the love of all the saints combined, is truly the sword of sorrow foretold by Simeon: a sword which plunges again and again into my soul during the Passion to mark it faithfully with all the Savior's sufferings, not only those of His body but also those of His mind, filled with reproaches, and of His heart, drowned in bitterness.

That is why the "Lamma sabacthani—Why have You forsaken Me," expressing the interior martyrdom of Jesus, makes my whole being shudder more violently than the blows of the hammer driving in the nails. Indeed that torture must have brought me death a thousand times if the same grace which associated me with the redemptive function of Jesus had not given me the strength to associate myself even to the end with His martyrdom.

Resolve, my child, to meditate often on my "Com-Passion." Seeing me turn my face and stretch out my arms and my whole being passionately toward the Crucified, you will be sweetly and irresistibly led to fix your gaze on those feet which let themselves be nailed that they might not tire of waiting for you, those arms which likewise let themselves be fastened to the cross that they might not tire of protecting you, that gaping side which was opened to give you passage to His Heart.

Seeing my soul broken with compassion in face of the sufferings of Jesus, you will be ashamed to look dry-eyed upon the Savior's wounds, and you will beg me to engrave them deeply in your heart as they are engraved in mine. Seeing my soul dissolving in love before that supreme devotion of Jesus, you will be ashamed at loving so little the One who loves you so much, and you will beg me to give you some part of my burning charity for the Savior!

> "Make my soul to glow and melt
> With the love of Christ my Lord."[7]

---

[7] Sequence *Stabat Mater.*

QUEEN OF CONFESSORS

MARY, MODEL OF ABANDONMENT TO GOD

THE ranks of the confessors, my child, include saints who have excelled in the most varied virtues and lived in the most varied states: Popes, bishops, religious, laymen, kings like St. Louis, beggars like St. Benedict Labre.

One trait, however, is common to them: their attaining holy abandonment, their achievement of complete acquiescence in God's good pleasure, imposing some trial or death itself on them. Next to martyrdom, this is the most decisive witness a man can bear to God's goodness and sovereignty.

Since in all the trials of my life and especially in the supreme trial of Calvary I practiced an abandonment more perfect and meritorious than that of all the saints together, it is quite right that I should be called Queen of confessors.

Certain saints *practice holy abandonment out of a love based on affection,* accepting trials or death as the surest means of being united to Jesus and enjoying His friendship.

My affectionate love for Jesus is incomparably more ardent and more intimate than theirs. Thus, when my dear Son is involved in the dreadful labyrinth of the five sorrowful mysteries, no force in heaven or on earth could prevent that love from drawing me after Him, my hand in His.

And I feel myself so much the more desirous of following Him to the very end in those five abysses of disgrace and sorrow because He has never appeared so lovable to me. Is not the Passion the supreme revelation of the Savior's lovableness! above all the supreme revelation of His love for men and especially for me! And am I not at His side to read with bodily and spiritual eyes the poignant declaration of love He writes with letters of blood in each of His wounds? Thus, far from detaching me ever so little from Jesus, His thorns and His nails by tearing my soul draw from it the last drops of tenderness I had not yet been able to give Him.

Other confessors abandon themselves willingly to trials and death *out of a love based on gratitude*: "Lord, we accept suffering and dying for Your glory because You have accepted suffering and dying for our salvation!"

That same love of gratitude to Jesus makes me acquiesce in all the stages of the martyrdom He asks me to undergo with Him.

My gratitude, however, is incomparably more perfect than that of other confessors. For I have incomparably more light to appreciate fully the benefit of the Redemption, more sensitivity to be moved and touched by it, more generosity to requite it unsparingly.

Again, having received more than anyone else from the divine Redeemer, I feel obliged to give Him back more than all others. Now what Jesus is doing under my very eyes is to pay through His sacrifice the price of my graces of preservation; the price of my graces of sanctification, greater than those of all the redeemed together; the price of those signal privileges that raise me above men and angels. At sight of this, how could my tender heart help dissolving in gratitude? How could it help urging me to give Jesus in return sacrifice for sacrifice, agony for agony, martyrdom for martyrdom?

Other confessors, the mystics above all, willingly accept trials and death *out of a love based on a right will*: to answer the Beloved's desire when He asks them to become victims with Him.

But who could have a greater hunger and thirst than I, to please Jesus and lend myself to His least desires? As High Priest He wants me to let myself be immolated with Him that He may offer me to His Father with His holy humanity as a single victim. As Redeemer of men He wants me to be associated with His sacrifice that I may be associated with His redemptive work and thus become the spiritual Mother of all the redeemed. With soaring heart and burning love I abandon myself to those adorable wishes of my Son and, in order to fulfill them wholly, I agree to share all the interior and exterior sufferings without asking dispensation from a single one.

Finally, other confessors deliver themselves to trials and death *out of a love blossoming in imitation*: their Master has given His life to glorify God and save souls; it is their need and their joy to do the same.

Here again my grace as Mother and Co-Redeemer allows me to desire more ardently that resemblance to Jesus suffering and dying and to make more fully my own the intentions that inspire His supreme sacrifice.

With Him I say to God, "Father, I love You with a love so extreme that I agree to deliver Jesus, my Life and my All, as a victim of adoration in recognition of Your supreme dominion over all creatures; as a victim of thanksgiving in acknowledgment that we have everything from You; as a victim of reparation to compensate for and prevent the horrible outrage of sin. And likewise I love mankind, Your adopted children, with such a love that I consent to deliver my dear Son to torture and death as a victim of propitiation that You may pardon their sins, as a victim of satisfaction that You may forgive them their debt, as a victim of impetration that You may grant them all the graces necessary for salvation."

Thus my abandonment to the divine will is the greatest burst of love the earth has ever sent up to heaven, after that of Jesus.

As I surpass all the other confessors in love, I surpass them also *in fortitude and in meekness.*

Throughout the Passion I say "Fiat—Let it be done" with unshakable constancy to each new aspect of the torment of Jesus, which is also my own: "Fiat" to each new blow of the scourge that tears His virginal flesh to shreds; to each new slap or expectoration that disfigures or soils His beautiful face; to each new blow of the stick that drives the cruel thorns a little deeper into His head; to each new blow of the hammer that makes the wounds in His hands and feet a little larger; to each new jibe thrown up to Him by His enemies; to my anguished powerlessness to wipe the sweat from His brow, the tears from His eyes, the blood from His wounds, to refresh His burning lips, to support His head which rests only on thorns, to mix the least drop of consolation into the flood of bitterness that fills His soul.

And when His lips breathe out to His Father the mysterious "lamma sabacthani," when His head drops on His breast to give His last gasp in a great cry, when the lance opens His heart to take the last drop of blood from Him, there is not a fiber of my being that does not acquiesce and consent! And I acquiesce with supreme meekness, without offering the least resistance, without uttering the least complaint against the men who are inflicting this agony on me or against God who is permitting it.

During the manifold trials of life, my child, and especially at the hour of death, you will have to imitate the divine Savior, who, after once imploring the removal of the chalice, does not tire of repeating, "Father, not as I will, but as You will!"[1]

It is clearer than day that, left to yourself, you are absolutely incapable of putting yourself in that attitude of abandonment and still less capable of persevering in it for long.

You should know, therefore, that it will become easy for you if at the first approach of a trial you take care to join me at the foot of the cross; to contemplate diligently my abandonment, so calm and so complete, and thus conceive the desire of imitating me; above all, to implore me diligently to obtain for you the fortitude and the constancy necessary for the realization of that desire.

> "By the cross with thee to stay,
> There with thee to weep and pray,
> This I ask of thee to give."[2]

[1] *Matt.* 26:39. [2] Sequence *Stabat Mater.*

QUEEN OF VIRGINS

MARY AND THE SOULS CONSECRATED TO GOD

I AM the Mother of the souls consecrated to God, because they have me to thank for the birth, preservation and fulfillment of their religious vocation.

To convince you of this, O consecrated soul, I need only remind you that I am the Dispenser of all graces, and that no one can either be called to the religious life or enter and persevere in it without an uninterrupted succession of graces.

First of all, my child, I merited and obtained for you *the grace of a vocation.* Responding to my desire, the eyes of Jesus rested on your soul to make you His spouse, whereas they passed over thousands of others without stopping—other souls just as capable as yours of knowing and loving Him.

Next I preserved that precious grace for you, in spite of all you could do to lose it. Not content to have surrounded you with the strong barrier of a Christian family and a Christian education, to have bidden the angels defend you against the ambushes of the world and the devil, I myself wanted to watch over you as a mother watches over her little one, re-

243

moving from your sight a fascination too disturbing, from your path a trap too menacing; carrying you, so to speak, in my arms to bring you safely over a dangerous passage. And if more than once you escaped my motherly arms, then, without considering your ingratitude, I did not grow tired of running to seek you, to pull you out of the ditch and to reconcile you with Jesus.

When the time came to follow Jesus, I untied with gentle fingers the external bonds that kept you in the world: family duties or the opposition of parents.

Was the obstacle in your own heart, trapped by the world's enticements? I freed you by showing you that even the most honorable life in the world often exposes the soul to terrible dangers, still more often to practical forgetfulness of God by forming a conspiracy of silence against Him, and always to an unavoidable partition, which would take away from God the best of your cares and affections to consecrate them to temporal concerns.

At the same time I inspired in you an ardent desire to follow Jesus by making you see in the religious life an oasis where the waters of grace flow abundantly through all the channels of prayer, sacraments, Mass, and where the constraint of rules, the exhortations of superiors and the example of other elect souls favor correspondence to those graces in a singular manner.

Having completed the novitiate, you had to bind yourself by *the three vows*. While your senses and your reason itself were dismayed in face of this weighty obligation, I obtained for you the grace of faith to let you see a great mercy in it. A chain, if you will, but a chain all made of love to attach you more closely to the sovereign Good. An amputation and a mutilation, if you will again, but an amputation that frees the soul from the suffocating growth of the evil inclinations, a mutilation that deprives the soul of certain natural goods (free disposition of one's possessions and one's activity, foundation of a home) only to enrich it with supernatural goods, incomparably more desirable. Instead of complaining, should not consecrated souls thank the Vine-dresser who prunes them more rigorously because He loves them more and wants them to bear better fruits?

Throughout your religious life I continue to show you the great advantage of each of the three vows.

When you suffer at seeing your *vow of poverty* deprive you of a great means of influence over men and even of the mere pleasure of helping them in their needs, I show you that it gives you great influence with God, an influence which allows you to procure for those you love, not fields, houses or income, but no less than a kingdom of glory and beatitude, the kingdom of paradise!

I show you also that if your vow of poverty deprives you of the pleasures, honors and independence given by wealth, it exempts you wholly from those heavy cares and grave temptations which beset the rich and make their salvation so difficult, as Jesus Himself says.

When you feel yourself bruised by the numerous shackles of *religious obedience,* I reveal to you the manifold advantages it procures.

Thus I reveal to you how it makes reparation for your sins. You have detracted from God's glory by taking a forbidden freedom. You restore it to Him by renouncing a freedom permitted.

I show you how it expiates your sins. The act of satisfaction must be both virtuous and penitential. Obedience makes your most indifferent acts as virtuous as itself, and it gives the most agreeable acts an element of penance by the constraint it involves.

I show you how religious obedience makes you avoid sin, both by preserving you from the most dangerous occasions— caprice, idleness, worldly associations— and by weakening the seven evil inclinations, of which sin is the natural fruit.

At the same time I show you how it enriches you with graces and merits.

It enriches you with graces; for to put yourself in the current of obedience is to put yourself in the current of grace, since God is too wise and too good not to accompany His orders or desires by all the graces required for their observance.

It enriches you with merits. By transforming everything into the service of God, obedience transforms everything into merit, even the most insignificant and least costly actions. And if there is question of works meritorious in themselves, it doubles their merit by adding to your poor offering of gold, frankincense or myrrh your most precious gift, the only one God forbids Himself to take by force: the gift of your free will.

Finally, when nature or the devil wants to make you homesick for human love, which you have renounced by your *vow of perpetual chastity,* I show you, as no one else could, that this vow wins for you an ideal Spouse, possessing all you can ever dream of.

What can your heart desire? Grace and beauty? Jesus is

the source of all beauty, and the very beauty that shines on the angelic countenance is but a pale reflection of His. Goodness? Jesus is the source of all goodness. He is Love itself, and any love you might find in a creature's heart would be only cold ashes compared to the affection with which He surrounds you. Glory and power? If you remain faithful to the very end, He promises to let you sit on His throne and to associate you in His royalty and His magistracy. Joy and happiness? No one else can give you anything but a partial, fleeting happiness. He is the only one who can satisfy all the hunger of your soul, the only one who can bring you into a place of eternal beatitude.

And even while awaiting that blessed day He reveals Himself to you in this exile as a Spouse more lovable than words can tell: a faithful Spouse, who does not forget and does not betray; a thoughtful Spouse, who offers you untiringly His possessions and His love, but without ever imposing them by force; an accommodating Spouse, who veils His glory so as not to dazzle your weak eyes, veils His grandeur to put Himself within reach of your embrace; a patient Spouse, who untiringly puts up with the blindness of your mind, the hardness of your heart, the inconstancy of your will; a compassionate Spouse, always ready to be moved to pity over your wounds or your troubles, even when they are your own fault; a merciful Spouse, more persistent in pardoning you than you are in offending Him; a tender and passionate Spouse, who gives you in Communion all that He has and all that He is, afraid of no extravagance that will bear witness to His love. So true it is that one gains all in consenting to lose all to follow Jesus!

Such are the precious truths, my child, which I always cause to be heard, understood and appreciated by the consecrated souls who cultivate devotion to me.

But if I am the Mother of knowledge, "Mater agnitionis," I am equally the Mother of pure love, "Mater pulchrae dilectionis." And so, at the same time that I obtain for consecrated souls the grace of enlightenment to show them the indescribable love of the divine Spouse, I obtain for them and dispense to them the grace of generosity to let them respond to that love by a similar love, pure, tender, devoted to the point of sacrifice. "I walk in the way of justice . . . that I may enrich those who love me, and may fill their treasuries."[1]

[1] *Prov.* 8:20,21; Common of feasts of the Blessed Virgin Mary, 1st nocturn, 2nd lesson.

QUEEN OF ALL SAINTS

MARY'S REIGN OVER THE SAINTS

T HE saints, my child, all recognize my twofold royalty: *royalty of preeminence* calling forth their admiration, *royalty of authority* winning their complete submission.

The first preeminence the saints admire in me is my *dignity as Mother of God.* On earth you find it hard to understand this teaching of the theologians: "From the fact that she is the Mother of God, the Blessed Virgin has, in a way, an infinite dignity."[1] In heaven the elect gain a clear perception of that incomprehensible greatness simply by seeing the unique love it wins me from the three divine Persons.

They see the Father love me as His favorite Daughter to whom He gives a share of inheritance (grace on earth and glory in heaven) greater than that of all the other children together. And indeed, having given me His own Son for my true Son, why would He not lavish all His wealth and all His tenderness on me?

They see the Holy Spirit cherish me as His Spouse through

[1] St. Thomas Aquinas, *Summa Theologica,* I, q. 25, a. 6 ad 4um.

whom He causes Jesus to be born to natural life and men to supernatural life; and also as His chosen sanctuary in which He perceives more beauty than in the whole grand temple of paradise.

As to the Word incarnate, they see Him lavish on me as His true Mother a truly filial tenderness, gratitude and deference. Because these sentiments spring from the most loving Heart that can be, they bring me a happiness without limit; but because they proceed also from the Person of the Word who makes them truly His own, they win for me an inconceivable and, in a way, an infinite honor, which amazes the saints.

Just as I surpass all the saints by my dignity as Mother of God, I *surpass them again by my functions* of Co-Redeemer and Mediatrix.

Among all the elect I am the only one who has the honor of collaborating in the great work of the Incarnation: morally by giving a consent which was decreed to be indispensable, physically by giving the incarnate Word all that an infant receives from its mother. I am the only one who has the honor of collaborating in the work of the Redemption. I am the only one God has chosen to be the spiritual Mother of all the redeemed and the official Dispenser of all His graces.

Finally, I surpass all the saints by the *transcendence of my privileges.* For my soul is the only one besides that of Jesus that was exempt from original sin, the only one immune to every attack of the concupiscences, the only one to live a long life without either sin or imperfection, consequently the only one to whom God can say, "You are all fair, My love!"[2]

[2] *Cant.* 4:7.

At the sight of those various transcendences revealed in the full light of heaven, the elect *cannot forbear crying out their admiration* and their rapture.

"Be our Queen," say the patriarchs, "for if we are the roots of the human race, you are its summit and flower!"

"Be our Queen," say the prophets, "for you conceived, carried, bore, and embraced in your arms and against your heart the Desired of the nations whom we merely caused to be glimpsed across a night of many centuries!"

"Be our Queen," say the Apostles, "for it was your intercession and your irresistible attraction that called down the Spirit and His gifts on us the day of Pentecost!"

"Be our Queen," say the martyrs, "for if we were able to triumph over the formidable Satan, it was because you had already bruised his head under your immaculate foot!"

"Be our Queen," say the confessors, "for while each one of us reproduces only some of the Savior's virtues, you alone reflect all of them with an incomparable brilliance!"

"Be our Queen," say the virgins, "for it was your example and your grace that caused the lily of perfect chastity to bud in our hearts!"

To this royalty of preeminence which wins me the admiration and praise of all the saints, God has joined a *royalty of authority,* a *royalty properly so called* which gives me the right to their obedience.

Wisdom prompted Him to do this. In order to put more beauty and harmony into creation and especially into the heavenly kingdom which is its finest jewel, a wise Providence makes it a rule to subordinate the inferior beings to the superior and to govern them by the superior. It was fitting, therefore, that He confer on me supreme authority over all the saints as the natural crown of the other supremacies He has given me over them.

Love prompted Him. Desirous of showing me His filial love and of showing angels and men that I am dearer to Him than anyone else, Jesus feels compelled to give me a share in those unique privileges which He shares with no one else. And is not a universal royalty one of those privileges?

Finally, *justice prompted Him* to make me Queen. If it is just, that Jesus reign over the kingdom of the elect because He has taken them one by one from the powers of darkness, is it not equitable that I be associated with that royalty, since I was associated with every stage of the conquest and all the sacrifices it cost?

Penetrated with respect for the sovereign authority with which God has invested me, all the elect have the *disposition to obey* not only my orders but even my least desires. And whereas the kings of earth can demand only the material execution of their laws, my subjects in heaven fulfill my least wishes with the full adherence of their mind, which judges them to be supremely just; with the full adherence of their heart, which finds them supremely lovable.

On the other hand, seeing that this royal power is given me not to punish my subjects but only to make them good and happy, that it is a royalty of mercy, entirely at the service of my function as Mother, they are eager to *recommend to me the distress of their brethren on earth.*

How numerous and fervent are the petitions to "pray for us" arising to me from every corner of the earth! But how much more numerous and fervent are the petitions to "pray for our brethren" arising to me from the elect in every corner of paradise! And what ardent gratitude is poured out of their souls when I come to the aid of their protégés, especially when I win them the privilege of going to their aid themselves, their hands full of blessings and miracles!

But it is above all *on their own account that the elect bear witness of their gratitude to me.*

Seeing quite plainly with what devotion I acquired the life of grace for them at the price of my agony on Calvary; with what condescendence I distributed it to them throughout their earthly existence, accommodating it to all their weaknesses; with what solicitude I preserved it for them or gave it back to them, despite their incorrigible childish rashness; with what patience I taught them to make it grow and bear fruit; above all with what inexpressible motherly tenderness I filled the threefold role of nurse, teacher and guardian— they thank God for having given them a whole eternity to thank me.

And now that they see that unique tenderness glow in my eyes and my smile; now that they see it spring directly, like a sweet flame, from my heart become transparent to their eyes, they keep sending up to me a magnificent symphony of gratitude and love, amplified and embellished by each new wave of the elect!

Rejoice, my child, to know that I am so well honored by the saints. Ask them to obtain for you a large share in their devotion. Give them the mandate of praising and loving me in your stead. Above all, strive to make your own that conviction, perseverance and generosity which they brought to my service when they lived on earth.

QUEEN CONCEIVED WITHOUT ORIGINAL SIN

MARY PRESERVED FROM ORIGINAL SIN

O N December 8, 1854, Pope Pius IX proclaimed solemnly and made it a part of your faith that at the first instant of my Conception I was preserved immaculate from all stain of original sin.[1]

My privilege consists essentially in this: while all the other children of Adam, through the sin of their first father, enter into existence deprived of supernatural life and receive it only on the day when they are baptized by act or by desire, *I alone received that precious supernatural life at the same time with natural life,* that is to say, at the very instant when God was creating my soul and uniting it to the body destined for it.

At first glance, my child, you do not comprehend the great misfortune of a soul's being deprived of that life of grace

---

[1] *Mary Immaculate,* the Bull *Ineffabilis Deus* of Pope Pius IX, translated and annotated by the Rev. Dominic J. Unger, O.F.M. Cap. (Paterson, N.J.: St. Anthony Guild Press, 1946), p. 21.

for some months; nor, consequently, *the signal favor of being enriched with it from the first moment* of its existence.

To understand it, compare the state of my soul from that first instant with the state of other souls before their Baptism.

In clothing my soul with *sanctifying grace* God confers on it a supernatural beauty, a reflection of the indescribable beauty proper to the divine Being. There is no disputing that if all the rays of beauty shining in the world of nature could be united into one cluster, they would display less brilliance and less attraction than this simple reflection of God's face on His creature.

The souls of Adam's other children are deprived of that heavenly beauty until Baptism. In God's plan they were supposed to be resplendent and radiant like glowing metal; but, because the flame of grace is not lighted in them, they remain without brilliance and without attraction in the eyes of the three divine Persons.

By pouring into my soul, from that first instant, *the virtue of faith, the gifts* of knowledge, understanding and wisdom, the Holy Spirit confers on it, at least in germ, the power of knowing God as He is in Himself and not only as He reveals Himself in His works; the power, at least in germ, of penetrating the inaccessible light where God dwells and contemplating the splendor of His infinite beauty face to face, without being blinded by it.

Adam's other children must await Baptism to be made capable of this mode of knowledge. And if it is a great forfeiture in human eyes for an adult to be deprived of the light of reason, it is a still greater forfeiture in the eyes of God and His angels for any soul to be deprived of the light of grace.

Always, from that first instant, by pouring *charity* into my soul, the Holy Spirit confers on it the power to be united without intermediary to its sovereign Good, infinite Beauty and Goodness, made accessible to its lowly embrace,[2] and also, the power to merit one more degree of glory and beatitude by each of its free acts.

In Adam's other children the forfeiture of supernatural life entails the forfeiture of that supernatural capacity for love and merit. As long as they have not received that capacity in Baptism they appear in God's eyes like a wild plant with its graft cut off, a source of mere indifference or aversion because it is found to be a useless, disgraceful encumbrance in an orchard.

The possession of grace from the first instant of my conception wins me many other advantages. Since it is a true participation in the divine nature and life, God *considers me* from that first instant *as His child* and extends to me the same fatherly affection and tenderness He has for His only Son.

Deprived of this divine life, Adam's other children are born "children of wrath."[3] They can be regarded and treated by God only as subjects, and moreover as subjects issued from a fallen father. For them, as a result, He could not have any other love than the compassionate love one has for outcasts.

Finally, the possession of grace from that first instant *allows me to enter on an equal footing into the glorious family of the angels* by making me participate, like them, in the divine life.

The privation of grace makes Adam's other children strangers to the heavenly spirits, with whom they no longer have

[2] St. Thomas Aquinas, *Summa Theologica*, IIa IIae, q. 27, a. 4 ad 3um.
[3] *Eph.* 2:3.

anything in common. What is more, it lets them fall under the sway of the devils as part of the spoils won by the latter for their first victory over the father of the human race; and it leaves them undefended against all the sallies of those impure spirits who, no longer kept back by the presence of the Holy Trinity, can enter at will into the temple of their soul to debase and profane it.

Thus the possession of grace from the first instant implies such great goods and preserves me from such great evils that it would still be an outstanding privilege even if the grace had been measured out sparingly.

Actually (and this crowns my privilege) God gives me *a measure of grace greater than that which He reserves for the angels and saints together.*[4] The reason is that, loving me as His true Mother, He loves me more than all of them together; and for God to love is not only to will the good but to give it.

It follows that, from the first instant, God discovers more beauty and takes more pleasure in my soul alone than in all the angels; and this disposes Him to bend over the earth with singular tenderness, despite the clamor of sin which the earth keeps sending up to Him.

How solemn, then, is that first instant of my existence! Out of the midst of the corrupted mass of the human race emerges a luminous peak, a virginal point, by which God is going to make contact again with sinful humanity. Out of the midst of the darkness of this world saturated with sin springs the glorious Dawn, messenger of the Sun of justice. In the silence of the night resounds a cry of victory: for

[4] Pius IX, *Mary Immaculate,* p. 2.

the first time God has removed an offspring of Adam from the clutches of sin and death; He has just struck His first blow on the jaw of the Evil One, to make him let go of his prey.[5]

It is written that the heavenly spirits shouted for joy when they saw the Creator "laying the foundations of the earth."[6] How much greater are their joy and admiration when they see Him bringing into existence her who is the masterpiece, the ornament, the Queen of all creation! God Himself cannot help expressing how pleased He is with me, and He proclaims me all fair on earth and in heaven: "How beautiful you are, My Love, how beautiful you are!"[7]

For me this mystery is dearest of all, because it calls forth the first kiss and the first embrace of infinite Love entering my soul to preserve it from all evil and enrich it with a fulness of grace. That is why those who honor me under the title of Immaculate give me great pleasure, for which I repay them with notable favors: consider the numberless prodigies of the miraculous medal, of Our Lady of Victory, of Our Lady of Lourdes!

Make it a habit, therefore, my child, to address to me always, but most particularly in time of temptation, the invocation "Queen conceived without original sin, pray for us!"

This will accomplish several things at the same time: put the devil to flight by reminding him of the one who crushed his head, deliver your soul from evil thoughts or desires by plunging it into a bath of light and purity, merit more effective help and protection from me.

[5] *Job* 29:17.   [6] *Job* 38:4,7.   [7] *Cant.* 4:1.

QUEEN TAKEN UP INTO HEAVEN

MARY'S ASSUMPTION

O N November 1, 1950, Pope Pius XII defined as a dogma of faith that having completed the course of my earthly life, I was assumed body and soul into heavenly glory.[1]

If the Holy Spirit has taken care to reveal this truth to mankind, He must consider it very important. And if at the present time He has introduced the infallible teaching authority of His Church as a guarantee of a true divine revelation, He must want to arouse people to a better knowledge and greater honoring of this glorious privilege. To help you achieve these goals, my child, I am going to explain the principal motives that prompted God to grant me without delay that glorification of the body which the rest of the elect will not receive until the final resurrection.

That glorification is demanded *by my dignity as Mother of God.*

---

[1] *Munificentissimus Deus,* translated by the Rev. Joseph C. Fenton (Washington, D.C.: National Catholic Welfare Conference), #44, p. 19.

Because I am His true Mother, Jesus surrounds me with a filial love so great that no one could conceive any more perfect.

Loving me with such a love, how could He help being impatient to procure the happiness of heaven for my body as soon as possible; and for my soul that completeness of beatitude which is involved in its reunion to the body?

Loving me with such a love, how could He stand having this virginal body, from which His own body issued, this motherly heart which always beat in rhythm with His, become the prey of worms, or at least remain far from His sight, without movement and without life, until the end of time?

The fact is that on earth, prompted by His filial love, Jesus jealously preserved my body from all the forfeitures not required by the Redemption. He even worked the great miracle of the virgin birth to spare it the slightest diminution. To be faithful to His plan and to His love, must He not spare it the humiliating, interminable captivity of the tomb?

He has the more reason for sparing it that captivity because persistence in the state of death until the second coming of Christ is the sign of Satan's victory over man and the effect of the anathema pronounced by God, "Dust you are and unto dust you shall return."[2] Could so loving a Son tolerate having His Mother subject to such a servitude and such an anathema?

The Assumption of my body is demanded also *by my Immaculate Conception.*

By the fact of original sin all the children of Adam are subjected to spiritual and bodily death. The Redemption delivers them from the first through Baptism, from the second through final resurrection.

----

[2] *Gen.* 3:19.

The privilege of my Immaculate Conception consists in this, that my soul was not delivered, but preserved, from spiritual death. And God has no reason for denying my body that favored, complete and preventive Redemption which He grants to my soul.

On the contrary, His justice demands that she who was exempt from sin and the inclination to sin in her body as well as in her soul, should also be exempt from the penalties of sin in her body as well as in her soul. And the penalty of sin for the body is to die and return to dust.

As to His wisdom, it may well permit me to "taste death"[3] in order to perfect my resemblance to Jesus; for the same reason it does not consent that I remain in the bonds of death.

Moreover, how could death hold her captive who is immune from all sin, when the Apostle assures us that death makes its appearance in the world and subjugates men only through sin: "The sting of death is sin!"[4]

The Assumption of my body is demanded *by my function as Co-Redeemer.*

I enjoy this title both for having given you the Redeemer and for having cooperated with Him in the whole extent of the redemptive work.

Is it not a demand of wisdom, then, that the new Eve should have the privilege, at the end of this life, of being glorified in body and soul, like the new Adam? Is it not a demand of justice that the Co-Redeemer share the final condition of the Redeemer rather than that of the other redeemed?

Actually the Scriptures, interpreted by Tradition, attest that

[3] *Heb.* 2:9.
[4] *1 Cor.* 15:56; *Rom.* 5:12.

I am to share the Redeemer's full triumph over Satan[5] and that this triumph involves a victory over sin through His expiatory sacrifice, a victory over death through His Resurrection and Ascension.[6] As I was associated in His victory over sin through my participation in the sacrifice of the cross, I must be associated also in His victory over death through my Assumption.

According to the Scriptures again, the Redeemer is to be the meritorious cause[7] and the exemplary cause[8] of your salvation. By taking part in the Passion of Jesus I merited for you in equity all that He was meriting for you in strict justice.[9] By participating in His Resurrection and Ascension I become for all of you a model and a pledge of the glorification reserved for your bodies at the end of time: a pledge the more certain as I am a mere creature like yourselves.

The Assumption of my body is demanded *by my dignity as Queen of men and angels and the whole universe.*

By consenting to the sufferings and humiliations of the Passion required by the redemptive plan, Jesus merited not only to be glorified but to be exalted body and soul above the heavenly spirits and every creature: "He became obedient to death. . . . Therefore God has exalted Him and has bestowed upon Him the name that is above every name."[10]

To serve the same plan the new Eve consented to undergo in her heart all the sufferings and humiliations of the new Adam. It is equitable, therefore, that she receive the same

[5] *Gen.* 3:15; Pius IX, *Mary Immaculate,* p. 14.
[6] *1 Cor.* 15:54-55.
[7] *Heb.* 5:9.
[8] *Rom.* 8:29.
[9] Pius X, *Ad diem illum.*
[10] *Phil.* 2:8-9.

reward: that she be exalted and that she also reign, body and soul, in heaven.

From another point of view, a royalty so perfect must exclude all dependence and all inferiority in relation to its subjects.

But if my body were still detained in the bonds of death, the Queen of the universe would be in a state of humiliating dependence on cosmic forces and even, in a sense, on the devil, of whom the Apostle says that he "holds the empire of death."[11]

If my body were not already glorified and beatified, would not the Queen of the angels be inferior, from this point of view, to the heavenly spirits already in possession of the fulness of happiness and glory destined for them?

Finally, my bodily glorification is particularly favorable *to the exercise of my spiritual motherhood.*

First of all, the knowledge that I am both body and soul in heaven makes it easier for you to picture my mother love in a tangible way, as you must in your condition of childhood. Thus without great effort you can contemplate my heart all vibrant with love for you, a love next to which all earthly loves are as cold as ice. You can see my eyes lowered toward you, full of compassion, and then raised to Jesus to obtain pardon and grace for you. You can see my hand ever poised over your soul to defend it against the tempter's violence or seduction, to support it when it stumbles, to lift it up again when it falls, to guide, draw and, if need be, carry it in the rugged path of virtue.

It is easier for you also to express your filial love to me.

[11] *Heb.* 2:14.

You can kneel in spirit at my feet to offer me your gifts and set forth your requests. You can hide in my arms to escape the attacks of the devil, who dares not follow you into this refuge. You can receive from my lips a reproach that makes you blush for your cowardice, but also a smile that comforts you in your troubles, reassures you in your anxieties, encourages you in your weariness, strengthens you when you are bending under a cross that is too heavy.

That is how my bodily Assumption is the normal outcome and complement of all my other privileges.

At the remembrance of this mystery rejoice, my child, that your gentle Mother in heaven, who has suffered so much for you, is now fully blessed and glorious in her body as well as in her soul.

Of the just who have risen, Jesus says that they "shall shine forth like the sun."[12] Now the glory of my body (like that of my soul, of which it is but the radiation) surpasses in brilliance the glory of the angels and the saints combined. Thus Bernadette, although she had glimpsed only a reflection of it, cried in ravishment, "She is so beautiful that when you have seen her once, you would want to die to see her again!"[13]

You should love to call up in your soul the image of that unequaled Beauty. It will drive from your soul everything that troubles, saddens or tarnishes it, and bring in purity, uprightness, peace and joy to reign there.

The remembrance of my glorified body should also inspire in you a keen desire to assure your own body the glorious resurrection Jesus merited for it.

[12] *Matt.* 13:43.
[13] Colette Yver, *L'Humble Sainte Bernadette,* p. 241.

To that end apply yourself, following my example, to surrounding your body with modesty and purity as the true temple of Christ and of the Trinity. Work at subjecting it and using it in the service of God and of your brethren as "a living sacrifice, holy, acceptable to God."[14] And in return God will confer on it for eternity such a measure of happiness and glory as will make you consider insignificant the heaviest burdens of work and suffering you have made it bear during its earthly pilgrimage.

[14] *Rom.* 12:1.

QUEEN OF THE MOST HOLY ROSARY

WHY WE MEDITATE THE MYSTERIES OF THE ROSARY

T HE first advantage of this meditation, my child, is to make you contemplate and *honor my three great privileges* in being Mother of God, Mother of men and universal Mediatrix.

The joyful mysteries present to your view in a most pleasant light all the aspects of *my divine motherhood.*

The mystery of the Annunciation reminds you how I really conceived the Man-God, thus becoming the beloved Daughter of the Father, the Mother of the Word, the Spouse of the Holy Spirit.

The Visitation reminds you how I alone possessed the sovereign Good of angels and men in an indescribable communion of nine months.

The Nativity reminds you how I brought Him into the world and surrounded Him with a mother love worthy of an Infant-God.

The Presentation reminds you how, in the name of the

human race whose flower and summit I am, I offered God the perfect fruit which my virginity brought forth.

The Finding of the Child Jesus reminds you how that loving Son reserved for me thirty of the thirty-three years of His life, surrounding me with a truly filial tenderness, solicitude and deference.

What could be more effective than these reminders to convince you that I am God's most beloved creature, the one who best reflects His beauty, goodness and power? What could more effectively inspire you with a profound veneration and unlimited admiration for me, an unquenchable thirst to know and love me always more?

The sorrowful mysteries remind you how I became the true *Mother of men* by associating myself, as the new Eve with the new Adam, in all the stages of the great immolation which gave you a rebirth into the life of grace: agony, scourging, crowning with thorns, carrying of the cross, crucifixion.

Every one of those mysteries reveals how much it cost me to bear you into supernatural life. Did I not have to feel all my dear Son's interior and exterior sufferings exactly as if they were my own: both the sting of the scourges, thorns and nails torturing His flesh, and the incomparably crueler sting of your sins afflicting His soul?

But by the very fact, those mysteries reveal also how much I loved you. For love of you did I not consent, in each of them, to having Jesus delivered to worse sufferings and humiliations? And to deliver Jesus in that way is to deliver myself.

It follows that you cannot go through those mysteries without crying at each step, "She loved us and delivered herself for us. Let us love her who has loved us so much!"

The glorious mysteries remind you that I am the *Mediatrix for men* with the supreme Mediator, Jesus Christ.

In the mysteries of the Resurrection and the Ascension you see me admiring the triumph of Jesus which I alone can understand, and offering Him in the name of the whole mystical body the only praise worthy of Him.

In the mystery of Pentecost you see me calling down on the Church the Spirit of holiness who is going to give it life and growth.

In the mysteries of the Assumption and the Coronation you see me penetrate into the light of God, where it is given me to know the desires and the needs of each of my children; into the power of God, where I receive the faculty of dispensing all the fruits of the Redemption to each one of you.

How can you contemplate me in these various functions of Mediatrix without feeling compelled to make all your acts of praise and petition pass through my hands?

The second advantage of meditation on the mysteries is to unfold frequently before your eyes, under the form of most attractive examples, *the complete program of Christian perfection.*

Jesus has summed up this program in three phrases: to renounce oneself, to carry one's cross, to walk in His footsteps.

In the joyful mysteries I teach you to *practice all the forms of renunciation*:

In the Annunciation, denial of sensuality and pride through purity and humility. See how I bear witness to my virginal purity above all: "How shall this be done?" See how I lower myself before God at the instant when He proposes that I become His Mother: "Behold the handmaid!"

In the Visitation, denial of selfishness through charity. See how I hasten to obtain joy of heart and holiness of soul for my relatives by carrying Jesus to them!

In the Nativity, renunciation of riches and comfort through poverty. See how I put up with stark privation for myself and my Son!

In the Presentation, denial of my own will through obedience. See how I subject myself to all the prescriptions of the Law, even those from which I could dispense myself!

In the Finding of the Child Jesus, renunciation of material consolations through submission to God's good pleasure. See how I seek the Beloved not to enjoy Him but to serve Him!

Yes, my child, give your mind's full attention and all your heart's love to considering how I practiced these various renunciations, and you will soon feel an irresistible urge to practice them yourself, despite any natural repugnance.

In the sorrowful mysteries, by acquiescing with an unreserved and persevering "fiat" to all the sufferings of Jesus, which are also my own, I teach you *the right way to carry every kind of cross*:

In the agony, the cross of compunction, which makes you weep bitterly for the outrage done to God both by your sins and by those of your brethren;

In the scourging, the cross of physical sufferings, even the cruelest and the least deserved;

In the crowning, the cross of humiliations, even the most ignominious, such as scoffing, blows and spittle;

In the carrying of the gibbet, the cross of duty: family, social, apostolic obligations, even when they bring you nothing but ingratitude and opposition;

In the crucifixion, the supreme cross of death, whatever may be its providential concomitants: persecution by men, apparent desertion by God.

Resolve, then, when you are oppressed by a trial, to consider how I carried my cross in each of these mysteries; that mere consideration will be more effective than any number of words in making you carry your cross with resignation, if not with love.

In the glorious mysteries I teach you to *achieve a more and more perfect union with Jesus*:

In the Resurrection, union with Jesus through the virtue of faith. When Jesus was dead I did not stop believing in His coming Resurrection or living with Him in thought and in affection.

In the Ascension, union with Jesus through the virtue of hope. When Jesus had left this world, I lived with the firm assurance that He was continuing to help me from the heights of heaven and that He would one day call me to Himself.

In the descent of the Holy Spirit, union with Jesus through charity. My whole life was but an uninterrupted sigh towards the Holy Spirit who alone can arouse and increase this virtue in the human heart.

In the Assumption, union with Jesus through a good death, a union which I desired and implored continually, because it is the only one that assures final and irrevocable possession of Jesus.

In the Coronation, union with Jesus through beatitude, the supreme good, for love of which I despised and repected as "dung" all the goods of this world.

Such are the different modes of union that brought me

progressively to the perfect possession of Jesus. The more you contemplate them in these glorious mysteries, the more you will be inclined to appreciate them, desire and implore them, and the more also you will render yourself worthy to receive the grace of those modes of union.

If you want to *adapt the meditation on the mysteries to the words* of the Hail Mary, my child, do it in this way:

In the first part of the Hail Mary, contemplate intensely the virtue proper to each mystery: "Hail, Mary; that is to say, I greet you, I admire you, I love you all shining with purity (in the Annunciation); all inflamed with charity (in the Visitation); hungry for that great justice which is humility (in the Nativity); etc."

In the second part, implore that virtue ardently: "Pray for us; that is to say, obtain for us that purity, that charity, that humility ... so desirable at all times and especially at the hour of death!"

That is a practice both salutary and easy. For nothing is so well suited to making you desire the virtues as to contemplate them incarnate and living in me; nothing is so effective in making you obtain them as to ask for them ten times in succession through me.

QUEEN OF PEACE

MARY AND PEACE AMONG NATIONS

THE Church calls me Queen of peace, my child, because she sees in me *a desire and a power unmatched by anyone, to make peace reign* on earth.

I am the most merciful of creatures: God Himself appointed me steward of His infinite mercy, with the mission of relieving all miseries.

How could I have anything but horror, then, for war, which turns loose on the human race such an avalanche of evils? What could I desire but to put an end to it, when I hear rising from every corner of the world the sighs of millions of families consumed by anguish; the sobs of millions of widows and orphans; the groans of millions of exiles; the anxious petitions of millions of human beings who feel death hanging over their heads; the harrowing cry of millions of wounded, their bodies pierced, crushed, burned; the death rattle of millions in agony, dying alone in the mud of the battle fields or under the rubble of the bombed cities?

I am the meekest of creatures: "Inter omnes mitis."[1] Must I not hold war in abomination, especially modern war which wrests from nature its most brutal forces, to make them fall again in a rain of steel and fire on the sick, on the aged, on women, on infants in their cradles?

I am the most loving of mothers; and all men, to whatever nation they belong, are my sons, my true sons, to whom I gave birth on Calvary into the life of grace, and whom I always surround with the affection of a perfect Mother. How could I help being moved to pity when I see them arrayed against one another and pursuing one another with homicidal fury on the ground, on the sea and in the air?

Finally, by associating me with His universal royalty Jesus has conferred on me a true sovereignty over all nations. How could I help being grieved to see those nations, all equally mine, drain their resources in goods and in men, not to help but to destroy one another?

Yes, no other creature in heaven or on earth can hate war as much as I, because no other has so clear a vision to compute the incalculable sum of evils it brings about, or so much compassion to feel those evils in all their poignancy, or so much charity to desire that the human race be preserved or delivered from them.

By what means can I realize this great desire and procure the reign of peace in reality?

The first instigator of wars is Satan. Irreconcilable enemy of God and of Christ, he takes his revenge for not being able

[1] Hymn *Ave Maris Stella.*

to do anything against Them by prompting men, children of God and members of Christ, to exterminate one another.

My function as Queen permits me to intervene, by myself or by the angels always at my service, to shorten the leash of that great enemy of peace, to prevent him from sharpening the spirit of ambition or greed in rulers, the spirit of hatred or vengeance among peoples.

Another instigator of war is the folly or greed of the heads of nations.

As Dispenser of all grace I can take away from their mind by a grace of enlightenment the firm persuasion that a certain war is required by their people's honor or vital interest; I can take away from their heart by a grace of uprightness the ambition or greed that induces them to prepare and unleash the conflict.

Still, since God could not permit one man's perversity to call down such a horrible scourge on the whole world, the *principal cause of war* must be sought *in the sins of all,* sins of peoples and rulers, sins of individuals, families and societies.

If God permits war, the real reason is that He sees in it a perfect aptitude to punish sin. War punishes undue attachment to riches by raging destruction; disordered attachment to comfort and enjoyment by unheard of privations and restrictions; culpable attachment to temporal joys and life by the worst physical and moral sufferings and a continual threat of death. Above all, it punishes pride by obliging man to chastise himself with his own hands and with the very things of which he is proudest: his strength, his courage, his discoveries, his social organization!

In God's plan, therefore, war is a chastisement designed to

punish the inquity of the human race when it reaches a certain level: "You shall drink the cup of desolation . . . you shall devour the fragments of it, and shall tear your breasts."[2]

Now I have great influence with God's heart to incline Him to shorten or remove that terrible sentence with which He threatens you through the mouth of His prophet: great influence with His mercy, which does not know how to refuse me anything because I am His Mother, all loving, all loved; great influence with His justice, which I can disarm by offering Him my propitiations of Calvary.

But in God's plan war is also a violent remedy, designed to cure ordinary souls of their guilty attachments, chosen souls of their fleeting attachments.

As Mediatrix of all grace I have the power of dispensing to sinful souls the spirit of repentance which will make them break their bad habits once and for all, however tyrannical they may be; to virtuous souls the spirit of generosity which, by making them carry in a Christian way the heavy cross of war time, will quickly raise them to the level of perfection on which God wants them. And God Himself hastens to put an end to a trial as soon as it has attained its purpose.

Convinced that I can dispense peace, like any other grace, "to whom I will, when I will, as I will," Pius XII has consecrated the entire human race to my immaculate Heart, that I may obtain this great favor for them: "Mother of mercy, *obtain for us the graces* which prepare, win and *assure peace."*[3]

But in order that I may obtain these precious graces for a people, the whole nation and its head must ask me for

---

[2] *Ezech.* 23:34.
[3] *Consecration of the Human Race to the Immaculate Heart.*

them with humility, confidence and perseverance; for, without this, God would draw no glory from His gift, not even the very modest homage rendered by prayer to His goodness and power.

Now very often men refuse to fulfill that condition. Sometimes, after a few days of supplication they grow tired of praying to me; and I must intervene myself, as at Pontmain, to rouse them from their apathy: "Well now, pray, my children!" Sometimes it is only an infinitesimal minority who think to implore my intervention, while the bulk of the populace, with their leaders at the head, continue to neglect or scorn supernatural means, preferring to rely only on human resources. Would it be just, would it be wise for me to obtain a quick triumph for them, when they would attribute all the glory of the victory to themselves and it would only confirm them in their pride and their irreligious secularism?

On the other hand, I never fail to hear the trusting, persevering supplication of a whole people and their rulers.

On his departure for the Crusade, St. Louis entrusts to me the fate of his kingdom.[4] I preserve it from all war, civil or foreign, during his long absence. In the darkest hours of the Hundred Years War, Charles VII and many other Frenchmen come to the shrine of Le Puy to recommend the fate of their country to me. I raise up for them a miraculous savior in the person of St. Joan of Arc, who herself has borne witness to me before her judges: "I came to the king of France ... in the name of the Blessed Virgin."[5]

[4] A. de La Francquerie, *La Vierge Marie dans l'Histoire de France,* p. 70.
[5] *Procès,* I, 175; *The Trial of Jeanne d'Arc,* translated by W. P. Barrett (New York: Gotham House, 1932), p. 126.

At the present time, my child, when exterior and interior peace remain precarious and cruelly threatened, unite yourself to the group of souls who keep asking my immaculate Heart to establish them in peace: "Funda nos in pace."[6] The Church herself invites you to do this through the voice of her Head: "The nations groan under the weight of divine chastisements and tremble for fear of still greater calamities.... Lift up your heart, then, to the Mother of God, in whom the Christian people have always sought refuge in time of danger, since she has been established as the cause of salvation for the whole human race."[7]

[6] Hymn *Ave Maris Stella.*
[7] Pius XII, *Ingruentium malorum.*

PRAY FOR US

WHY SHOULD WE CALL UPON MARY?

TO each title of praise in the litany the Church makes you add this supplication: "Pray for us."

In the first place, my child, why do you make *a plea so short and so vague?*

It is good, ordinarily, that you explain all your troubles to me in detail, to relieve them by pouring them out into my motherly heart; all the wounds of your soul, to become more vividly aware of them and eager for their healing.

But sometimes it is good also to trust yourself simply, like a little child, to my wisdom and my mother love, being content to call me to your aid: "Pray for me," that is to say: occupy yourself wholly with me, like a mother with her newborn baby; minister to all my needs, which you know better than I!

Why, moreover, should you *repeat this appeal for help so often,* since you are assured beforehand of my attention and my compassion?

In the mind of the Church the purpose of this repetition

is to inspire in you a more lively desire for my assistance and my protection by reminding you of your destitution and help-lessness, like that of a little child in face of a need or a danger, who has no other resource than to keep crying for its mother.

This repetition has also the purpose of awakening or en-livening in you the compunction which befits a sinner and a waster of graces. By constraining yourself to knock many times on the door of my heart, you are repairing the outrage you have done me in letting me knock in vain, many times, on the door of your heart!

Moreover, far from shaking your filial confidence, this repetition cannot but increase it. For it gives you the im-pression of recasting your prayer each time, to purify it always more of its habitual dross: lack of attention, respect and warmth; it gives you the impression of clothing it again, each time a little more, in that humility and filial confidence which make it worthy of being heard.

To be sure, your senses and your imagination are sometimes annoyed at seeing themselves bound to an occupation always the same. But your soul, which so many Communions have made a sharer in the dispositions of Christ, resembles the In-fant Jesus. Like Him, it tastes a secret happiness in thus pro-longing its unwearied conversation with me, in being sheltered as long as possible in my arms, its favorite refuge, in reposing as long as possible on my motherly heart, there to drink the sweet milk of grace which it is my mission to dispense.

Finally, why do you give supplication alone *more place* than all the other duties together: praise, veneration, thanks-giving, love?

First, to recur often to my intercession is an *easy means of glorifying me.* Always preoccupied with yourself, you are hardly ever inclined to praise and thank me; on the contrary, the feeling of your powerlessness or your distress, which seldom stops pressing on you, inclines you to cry frequently to me.

Now this prayer implies a glorfiication that is indirect but very real. To pray to me is to confess that I can do that which you cannot and, consequently, to pay homage to my power; it is to recognize that I am disposed to obtain all sorts of favors for you and, consequently, to pay homage to my compassionate goodness.

In the second place, frequent recourse to my intercession is an *easy means of giving me great joy.* What it does is to lead you to hold frequent conversation with me, to confide in me your fears, your troubles, your faults, and thus to tie yourself more intimately to me every day; and what could be more desirable for my motherly heart?

But what I desire still more is to be able to pour out on your soul graces which enlighten, console or protect, purify or sanctify. And the more you realize that condition put by God, "Ask and you shall receive," the more broadly you permit me to exercise this power.

Above all, to have frequent recourse to my intercession is to *bring great profit to yourself* by assuring yourself of the support of my prayer, a support always useful and often indispensable.

The fact is that God often refuses to listen to your supplications because there is question of surpassing graces (for example, gifts of the Holy Spirit, effective graces) to which you have no claim at all; or graces of which you have made yourself absolutely unworthy through prolonged abuse. Still more often God refuses to listen to you because your prayer itself is so impeded by lukewarmness or evil inclinations that it does not succeed in achieving that minimum of attention and desire, confidence and humility, without which it cannot be taken into consideration. Then you can apply to yourself the terrible threat, "You shall cry to Me and I will not listen to you!"[1]

What are you to do in such grave circumstances if not have recourse to her whom God has appointed your advocate and your refuge against His very justice?

It is true that you come to me disfigured with a thousand stains. But I am light, and the light does not fear to be soiled by the mud; I am Mother, to a degree which God alone can comprehend, and a mother never lets herself be repelled by the sores of her little one, however hideous they may be.

It is true too that you do not know how to converse with me, and that your petitions to "pray for us" include as many distractions as supplications. But does not a mother know how to interpret her little one's babbling?

It is true, finally, that you ask me for deliverance from temptations provoked by your own imprudence; for the healing of tryrannical habits which are the fruit of your numerous faults; for spiritual or temporal benefits of which you have often made ill use. But has anyone ever seen a mother hesitate to pull her little one out of the ditch because he fell into it through his own fault? refuse to bandage his hurts

[1] *Is.* 1:15; *Jer.* 11:11; *Ezech.* 8:18.

because they are the result of his disobedience? deprive him of bread because he happens to waste it?

Being your true Mother, I have always the desire of obtaining all pardons and all graces for you. Being Mother of God, I have always the power.

Only the angels and the saints can understand the extent of my influence. You may get some idea of it, however, by considering that Jesus is the most loving and the most grateful of sons and that, in order to show me His filial fondness and gratitude, He hastens to fulfill my least desires.

To be sure, Jesus ordinarily requires that these graces be properly desired and implored. And you desire them very little! And you implore them very badly!

But, even though your desire be but a spark without brilliance or warmth, it suffices to make that brilliant, ardent flame which is the desire of my mother heart flare up. And even though your plea drags itself like a wounded bird in the rut of your worldly concerns, its effect is to set free another plea which will mount straight and swift as the eagle's flight, even to the throne of grace.

To be sure, again, you have no right to those spiritual and temporal favors which I ask for you; often you are even positively unworthy of them.

Nevertheless, God does not hesitate to grant them to me, not only because He wants to give me pleasure but also because He sees that I have merited them, through Jesus and with Jesus, at the price of a whole life of labor and suffering.

Do not grow weary, therefore, my child, of addressing to me those repeated petitions, "pray for us," which maintain and enliven your filial confidence and affection; which permit me to transmit your supplication to God, indescribably embellished and increased in value by the addition of mine; which give me the mandate of obtaining for you all the graces necessary to sanctify every hour of your life and especially the decisive hour of your death; which, finally, for all these reasons, bring me immense pleasure, as St. Alphonsus justly teaches: "Of all devotions, there is none so pleasing to our Mother as that of having frequent recourse to her intercession."[2]

[2] *The Glories of Mary*, part 5, 9th practice, p. 612.